UNITED STATES POWER SQUADRONS' BOATING COURSE

Supplement to the Video

UNITED STATES POWER SQUADRONS' BOATING COURSE

Supplement to the Video

Adapted from the United States Power Squadrons' Boating Course

Hearst Marine Books
New York

It is the policy of William Morrow and Company, Inc., and its imprints and affiliates, recognizing the importance of preserving what has been written, to print the books we publish on acid-free paper, and we exert our best efforts to that end.

ISBN 0-688-09126-1

Printed in the United States of America

First Edition

19 18 17 16 15 14 13 12

CONTENTS

Subjects that are listed in italics are covered in the video only.

WELCOME ABOARD!

This new six-lesson United States Power Squadrons Boating Course is the first video edition of a nationally recognized boating course which, to date, has taught three million Americans the essential ingredients of seamanship and boating safety.

The eighty-minute tape and accompanying book cover all the material normally conveyed in six weekly classes. Some of the material, such as *Navigational Aids,* will be relatively easy to memorize. Other subjects, such as *Piloting* and *The Marine Compass,* will require more study and practice.

SUGGESTIONS ON HOW YOU SHOULD TAKE THIS BOATING COURSE

This USPS Boating Course Video and accompanying book are divided into six corresponding sections. We recommend that you study one section at a time—first watching the video, then reading the corresponding section in the book. The book is called a supplement because it provides additional material not covered in the video that will help you answer the study questions and pass the exam.

Although the video and book contain all the information needed to pass the course, we also recommend that you read the relevant pages in Chapman's. You'll find an appendix in the back of the course book listing the references to Chapman's by page number. Once you have a thorough knowledge of a given section, answer the study questions in each section using a pencil so that you can erase incorrect answers. Check your results against the correct answers listed at the end of the book. If you score well, go on to the next section. If you do not, repeat the section until you understand it.

When you have completed the entire course and are ready to take the USPS exam, call the USPS 24-hour, 7-days-a-week toll-free number, 1-800-828-3380 (except in North Carolina, where the number is 919-821-0281, Monday through Friday, 8 A.M. to 4:30 P.M. E.S.T.). Tell the operator that you are interested in obtaining the telephone number of the Power Squadron member nearest to you. The member you call will arrange for you to take the USPS Boating Course Exam. If you pass (and the exam is based on your knowledge of the material in the course) you will be provided with a USPS Boating Course Completion Certificate, which you may offer as evidence to prove a rudimentary knowledge of boating. Please bear in mind that although USPS has approximately seventy thousand members in 442 squadrons located in most boating regions of the United States, Puerto Rico, the U.S. Virgin Islands, and other, more distant areas, it is possible that you may reside hundreds of miles from the nearest member.

The United States Power Squadrons is the largest private boating organization in the United States. It is nonprofit, nonmilitary, and nongovernmental and has been honored by three

United States presidents for its significant contributions to boating safety over the years. USPS began at the Boston Yacht Club in 1914 and in 1989 it celebrated its seventy-fifth anniversary. USPS assisted in the formation of the Canadian Sail and Power Squadrons, a similar organization that operates throughout most of Canada. USPS National Headquarters is located at 1504 Blue Ridge Road, Raleigh, North Carolina 27607.

RELATED COURSE MATERIAL

In the Event you do not already own the piloting tools needed for the home study work connected with this course, we recommend that you send for the *USPS Boating Course Piloting Kit* containing navigational tools that could not be packaged with the video. The kit, which costs $26.00, contains a USPS Plotter, a pair of USPS dividers, a hard-lead charting pencil, and the full USPS Boating Course textbook. The kit can be ordered by calling the USPS 24-hour, 7-day-a-week toll-free number, 1-800-367-8777 (except in North Carolina, where the number is 919-821-0281, Monday through Friday, 8 A.M. to 4:30 P.M. E.S.T.) and charging the $26.00 cost to your Visa or MasterCard account. Please allow two to three weeks for delivery. You can also order the kit by writing to United States Power Squadrons, P.O. Box 30423, Raleigh, North Carolina 27622. There is an order form included in this package. Your check should be made payable to USPS. In North Carolina, please add $1.50 sales tax. If you order by mail, please allow four to six weeks for delivery. Prices subject to change without notice.

We also recommend that you purchase *Chapman Piloting, Seamanship and Small Boat Handling* by Elbert S. Maloney and published by William

Morrow and Company. Well known as "The Bible of Boating," Chapman's is available in all major bookstores and marine dealers. It contains valuable additional information on each of the six boating course sections and the relevant page numbers are given at the end of this book. Chapman's also contains a wealth of boating information that is not contained in the basic USPS Boating Course.

SECTION 1

Boat Handling and Elementary Seamanship

DOCKING AND UNDOCKING

In docking and undocking a boat you must take wind and current conditions into account. Approach the dock slowly with just enough speed to maintain rudder control and maneuver the boat so that the crew can hand or toss a line ashore.

Even sailors use the engine to go to a gas dock because there is often considerable traffic. The approach is made at low speed and ideally against the wind and/or current. The boat is more maneuverable against the wind than with the wind pushing it in to the dock. The planned approach tells the skipper on which side to put fenders and dock lines. Approach the dock at an angle but, before hitting it, swing parallel to it as the boat glides to a halt.

Leaving the dock is also influenced by wind and current. A boat facing into the wind can be pushed off and moved ahead slowly toward a broad turn. With a boat under 25 feet, and wind astern, it is usually possible to push the stern away from the dock, then reverse enough to clear the dock.

If the wind is onshore (toward the dock),

move slowly forward against the bow spring line and steer toward the dock; this will move the stern away from the dock. For more on docking procedures, see Chapman's, pp. 200–209.

ADVERSE CONDITIONS

Adverse conditions include anything that spoils your boating day. Some of the more common troubles include running out of fuel or into bad weather, high wind and/or waves, collision, and running aground.

OUT OF FUEL

This can be a serious problem for a powerboat if help is remote or the weather is bad. Intelligent planning is the best defense. A skipper who knows tank capacity and rate of use (gallons per hour) at cruising speed can calculate the expected running time for full tanks. Estimating the effects of wind and currents along the route, he can determine how many miles he will cover in that time. Then playing it safe by committing only three fourths of the tank capacity, he calculates how many miles he can go without fear of exhausting fuel. Half the distance would be a prudent radius outward bound.

WEATHER

Bad weather at sea can generally be avoided by listening to a weather forecast. A frequently encountered (and difficult to predict) weather problem for a boater is reduced visibility. When visibility begins to deteriorate, take the following actions:

1. SLOW DOWN! You should be able to stop in less than half the distance you can see.
2. Determine your position as accurately as possible. If there are aids to navigation, identify the nearest. Refer to your chart and approximate your position.
3. Determine the course to your destination. Keep track of your position as closely as you can and estimate your time of arrival. If possible, run from one navigation aid to the next in preference to taking a shortcut across an unmarked body of water.
4. Post a lookout. If only one is available, post him or her as far forward as is safe.
5. Sound the required signals (see "Navigation Rules") and listen for the sound signals of other boats.
6. Turn on your navigation lights.
7. If you become lost, with no reasonable idea of your location, anchor if possible and wait for conditions to improve.

WIND, WAVES, AND CURRENT

When waves and wind are high the wisest course is not to go out. A cold or wet day is no fun. But what *if* you are caught in rough weather in spite of every precaution? First you should reduce speed and head the boat into the waves at a slight angle. The danger to avoid is broaching, being turned sideways to the waves which can lead to capsizing. Another hazard is swamping which can occur when your stern faces the waves. Do not reduce speed too much as you will find your steering control is decreased. It goes without saying that everyone on board should be wearing a life jacket (personal flotation device).

Wind and current both cause leeway, driving

the boat off its course. The course must be modified to take that effect into account.

COLLISION

This is the chief cause of accidental injury afloat. Collisions occur under the best of weather conditions almost always due to inattention on the part of the helmsman or lookouts. Keeping a sharp lookout at all times is a must in these days of high speed boats and dense traffic; accident situations develop quickly, and they must be anticipated and dealt with quickly.

If a collision occurs, you should immediately count your crew to determine if anyone is missing. Administer first aid to the injured if possible. Then quickly survey the damage to determine if the boat will stay afloat. Do everything you can to keep the boat and people afloat. Signal for help if there are other boats around or request aid over the radio. At the first opportunity, report the accident to the proper authority as regulations require.

If you come upon a collision scene, you are required to stand by if it is safe to do so, assist if possible, and back up radio calls for aid. Your first responsibility is to your own vessel and the people aboard, however, and you should not stand by if it is dangerous to do so.

GROUNDING

Almost every new boater will sooner or later have the unfortunate experience of running aground. Recreational boating often begins in protected, shallow waters and sooner or later the helmsman gets off course. If you are in a powerboat, there is a universal no-no that must be remembered when you go aground. The natural instinct is to reverse the engine and rev it up. Don't do it! Before the engine can be effective it may suck in large samples of the bottom with the cooling water. The resulting damage can be memorable.

Grounding is as serious as the speed with which the boat hits the bottom. Always check the hull for damage before attempting to get off and starting on your way again. If the grounded vessel is subject to wave action, serious damage can result from pounding. If it is a matter of the boat's bow being caught in the mud or sand in quiet water, a small boat may be freed by a couple of hands going over the side and pushing. But never go over the side unless you know how you can get back aboard. Larger, heavier boats and deep-draft sailboats require other measures. If one end of a boat is aground, shift weight to the other end. Rock the boat to release the suction seal of a soft bottom. Any method of shifting weight from side to side or fore and aft will help.

If the boat cannot be pushed off, perhaps it can be pulled off by kedging (see p. 18) or towing. Towing is preferable if you can get help from another craft but it can be dangerous and must be done right. First you must have a towline of sufficient length and you need to get it from one boat to the other, a feat sometimes calling for ingenuity. The towline should be at least twice the length of the towing boat. For safety's sake, the towline should be attached to something solidly a part of each boat. Beware of cleats that are held to the deck only by screws; they may pull out under strain. Deck hardware must be bolted through and reinforced with a back plate if it is to be used in towing. That distributes strain away from the small spot of deck where the cleat is seated.

Some towing craft have eyebolts on the transom for towing skiers. Loop a line through those eyes to make a bridle. Then attach the tow rope at the midpoint of the bridle and the boat will pull while staying on a straight course. Be sure that all parts of the rig are clear of the propeller.

Sailboats usually can take towing strain at the base of the mast, but to maintain straight direction, the towline must be led to the stern and lashed there.

Everyone, on both boats, should stay clear of the towline, in case a cleat or eyebolt pulls out.

For more information on towing procedures, see Chapman's, pp. 250–251.

MAN OVERBOARD!

This adversity calls for preparation and practice. As soon as an alarm is raised that someone has gone over the side, two things are imperative: The victim must be kept in sight and a flotation device thrown to mark the spot and help the victim stay afloat. Assign someone to keep the victim in sight and keep pointing to him at all times.

The helmsman meanwhile should head the boat back to the victim. A powerboat can simply make a 180-degree turn and head toward where the spotter points. A sailboat may come about and sail in the direction, or it may drop sails and motor back.

Approach from downwind and move alongside into the wind for the pickup. An approach from windward could result in the person being run over by the boat if it is blown by the wind. Ignore current; there is no relative speed. When almost alongside, stop the engine in gear to lock the propeller. A "wind-milling" prop can slash the victim's legs, which invariably swing up under the boat.

Then the task of recovery can begin. Take care in a small boat to keep it in trim. If everybody rushes to one location the concentrated weight may capsize the boat. Getting aboard a high-sided boat is not easy. The swimmer cannot raise himself to deck level. For those on the deck, who have to bend over the gunwale to help him, he is a heavy sack without a handle and they cannot use their powerful leg muscles in raising him. This is the moment for a boarding ladder or a swim step. A bosun's chair or line looped like one may bring him up, especially if there is a handy winch to take on the load. But if the victim is weakened, then a strong swimmer in a life jacket and with a lifeline will have to go overside to assist him. See Chapman's, pp. 248–249.

MEDICAL EMERGENCIES

The universal defense against injury when medical help is not at hand is the first aid kit and someone aboard who knows what to do with it. Take a first aid course for your own protection.

A medical crisis encountered frequently in boating is hypothermia, an abnormal lowering of the body temperature due to loss of heat from exposure to cold air, wind, or water. It probably kills more people than drowning does in marine accidents.

The condition results from two things: long exposure to cold with insufficient clothing on (chronic) or sudden immersion in cold water (acute). Water drains body heat twenty-five times faster than air does, so hypothermia can occur in as little as ten or fifteen minutes. While in the water the body can conserve heat with protective clothing as well as by remaining still, holding the thighs up to insulate the groin area, keeping the arms to the sides, and if possible, remaining close to another person and covering the head.

Symptoms of hypothermia are shivering,

mental disorientation, bluish skin and lips, incoherent speech, or unconsciousness. In fact, if the victim is very cold, suspect hypothermia. Some actions that you might normally take to fight cold can actually cause harm in the case of hypothermia. You should not, for example, massage the extremities or administer hot drinks. Learn the proper first aid procedures before you leave and if you encounter hypothermia get the victim to a physician as soon as possible.

HARMFUL EXHAUST

Carbon monoxide is the colorless, odorless gas that is the by-product of any internal combustion engine and can be a threat to boat passengers. If a vessel is running downwind slower than the wind speed, fumes from motor exhaust may blow forward into the cockpit and can cause seasickness or have a more dangerous effect.

ANCHORS AND ANCHORING

Anchors are marine tools with a long history. Bronze Age sailors used them and today's manufacturers are forever seeking new designs. An anchor's holding power depends on a combination of its weight and its ability to hook into the bottom. Here are the different types:

The kedge is also called the yachtsman's anchor. It may not stow readily on a small craft, but if your boat is big enough to carry one, it could also help you in a grounding. "Kedging" a boat off when it is aground works like this: Row the anchor with its line (the anchor rode) to a spot behind the boat. Lower it and set it by hauling on the rode. When it is set, try to winch in the anchor rode. This pull may free the grounded boat.

The Danforth is a popular anchor and is most

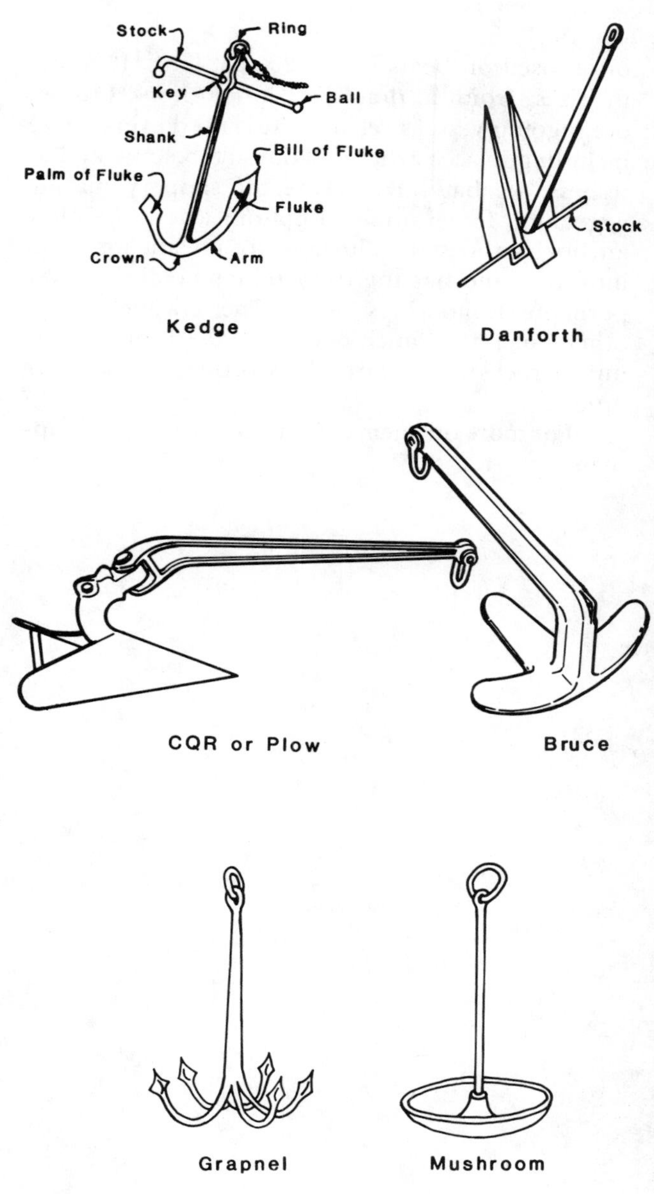
Stock
Ring
Key
Ball
Shank
Bill of Fluke
Palm of Fluke
Fluke
Crown
Arm
Kedge
Stock
Danforth
CQR or Plow
Bruce
Grapnel
Mushroom

Figure 1-1

often used on boats under 25 feet long. It comes in sizes from a dinghy's "lunch hook" to an oceangoing vessel's reliance. It is used everywhere including places where it doesn't belong and is useless. Its flat flukes skate off slippery marine vegetation for example, a bottom where the plow anchor is the star. The mushroom anchor sinks into mud and has the tremendous holding power permanent moorings need. The grapnel is another small boat lunch hook. It is used for anchoring in rocks but is virtually worthless in sand or mud.

For more on anchors and anchoring, see Chapman's, ch. 12.

Section 1: STUDY QUESTIONS FOR BOAT HANDLING AND ELEMENTARY SEAMANSHIP

1. Which of the following statements is **not** true regarding boat fuel and fueling?

   (a) Gasoline fumes are heavier than air.
   (b) Fuel tank vent pipes must be attached to the top of the tank.
   (c) Portable tanks are to be put on the dock for filling.
   (d) Gasoline evaporates quickly so spillage need not be wiped up.

2. If conditions permit, the preferred direction to approach a dock is:

   (a) against the wind or current—whichever is dominant.
   (b) down wind or current so a stern line can be passed ashore easily.
   (c) with wind/current onshore so vessel is blown right up to the dock.
   (d) with wind/current offshore so there is little chance of striking the dock.

3. When preparing to dock a boat:

   (a) have the crew stand by with fenders until you are alongside the dock.
   (b) come alongside the dock, then decide how long a dock line is needed.
   (c) instruct the crew, place the fenders, and have dock lines ready.
   (d) none of the above.

4. When getting under way from a dock:

   (a) always leave bow first.
   (b) with wind/current onshore, swing the stern out by going ahead against a bow spring line.
   (c) with wind/current ahead, go ahead at half throttle and steer away from the dock sharply.
   (d) regardless of wind/current, have someone on the dock push the boat out with a boathook.

5. Of prime importance in safe docking and undocking of a boat is:

   (a) judging the effect of wind or current on the boat.
   (b) having large fenders to prevent damage to your boat.
   (c) giving instructions in a loud authoritative tone so the crew will know who is in charge.
   (d) plenty of speed.

6. When docking a boat alongside a dock:

   (a) if a single-engine boat, dock starboard side to if possible.
   (b) approach with plenty of speed and then shift into reverse smartly.
   (c) approach slowly with just enough speed to maintain rudder control and maneuver the boat so the crew may hand or toss a line ashore.
   (d) none of the above.

7. A small boat turned sharply at high speed may result in:

   (a) capsizing.
   (b) loss of control.
   (c) throwing a person overboard.
   (d) all the above.

8. Adverse conditions can include:

   (a) bad weather; high winds and waves.
   (b) collisions and grounding.
   (c) running out of fuel.
   (d) all of the above.

9. After a pleasant day on the water, you start for home. A ground fog begins to build, reducing visibility to about half normal. Among other things, you would:

   (a) speed up to get home before it gets darker.
   (b) determine your position as accurately as possible and reduce speed.
   (c) continue course and speed, but turn on navigation lights.
   (d) continue course and speed, but post a lookout.

10. The most frequent cause of boating injuries is collisions. Most occur because of:

   (a) darkness.
   (b) bad weather.
   (c) lack of operator attention.
   (d) all of the above.

11. You have come upon a friend whose engine has failed and the cause cannot be determined. You agree to tow him to port. You have an appropriate sized line which should be made fast:

   (a) to his bow cleat and your port side stern cleat.
   (b) to his boweye and your starboard side stern cleat.
   (c) to his boweye and your towing eyebolts in the transom using a bridle.
   (d) none of the above.

12. When high winds and seas are encountered:

   (a) have everyone don life jackets.
   (b) if possible, turn to take the waves broadside to avoid excessive pounding.
   (c) if possible, head into the waves at a slight angle.
   (d) both a and c.

13. Hypothermia:

   (a) is the abnormal lowering of the body's internal temperature.
   (b) calls for giving the victim hot drinks.
   (c) should not be suspected if a person is cold, shivering, and has bluish skin.
   (d) should be treated by warming the person's arms and legs.

14. In case of a man overboard you should:

(a) approach the person slowly from windward.
(b) approach the person slowly from downwind.
(c) as you come alongside, keep your engine running.
(d) stop the boat and wait for the person to swim to it.

15. Carbon monoxide:

(a) is an odorless, colorless gas.
(b) is extremely toxic.
(c) can come back into the cockpit on long downwind runs.
(d) all of the above.

16. You have a boat 30 feet long with a beam of 8 feet. The draft is 3 feet. The height of bow is 4 feet. You decide to anchor in a protected cove for lunch. The chart shows a soft bottom (mud) in 10 feet of water. How much anchor rode should be put out to have a 5:1 scope?

(a) 70 feet.
(b) 50 feet.
(c) 20 feet.
(d) 85 feet.

17. The effect of a rising tide on the scope of an anchor rode would be:

(a) of no effect.
(b) to lessen it.
(c) to increase it.
(d) to reverse its direction.

18. An anchor's holding power depends on its:

(a) weight and ability to hook into the bottom.
(b) material of construction.
(c) width at the stock.
(d) all of the above.

19. The type of anchor likely to suit most needs of boats under 25 feet long, assuming its weight is appropriate, is the:

(a) grapnel.
(b) kedge.
(c) Danforth.
(d) mushroom.

20. The anchor that provides the most resistance to breaking out when the boat swings 180° is the:

(a) plow or CQR.
(b) Bruce.
(c) Danforth.
(d) all the above are about equal.

21. You are purchasing an anchor rode. The characteristics that are desired include:

(a) ability to be stored wet without deterioration.
(b) ability to float so it will not get into the propeller.
(c) resistance to stretch so the scope will remain the same.
(d) a hard, durable surface to resist being scuffed by the bottom.

22. Normally the scope of an anchor rode for most conditions is:

(a) 7:1
(b) 10:1
(c) 5:1
(d) 3:1

BOATING TERMS

Boating has a vocabulary all its own and since the study questions use these words and expressions it would be well to be familiar with them. Probably all of them appeared somewhere in the video lessons but the labels in the following figures group them for easy reference. And there is a bonus: Knowing the language, you won't sound like an alien when talking to more experienced people at the marina or around a yacht club.

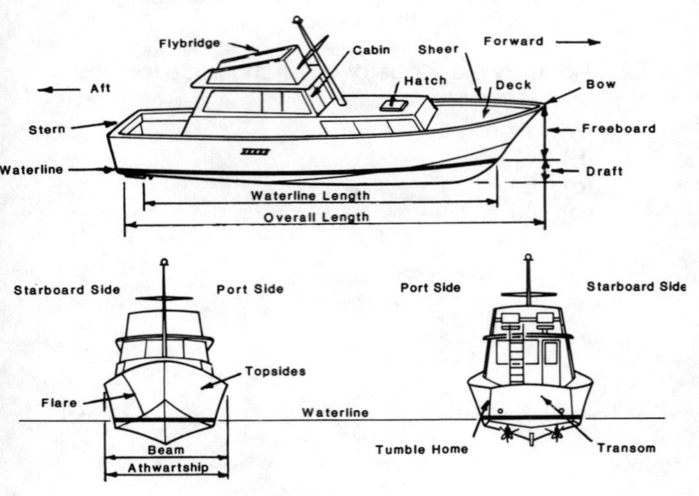

Figure 1-2

BOAT TYPES

Being able to identify craft is important because navigation rules differ for various types. The first distinction is between sail and power-driven boats. Powered craft as a rule carry no masts, although a sailboat running on its auxiliary

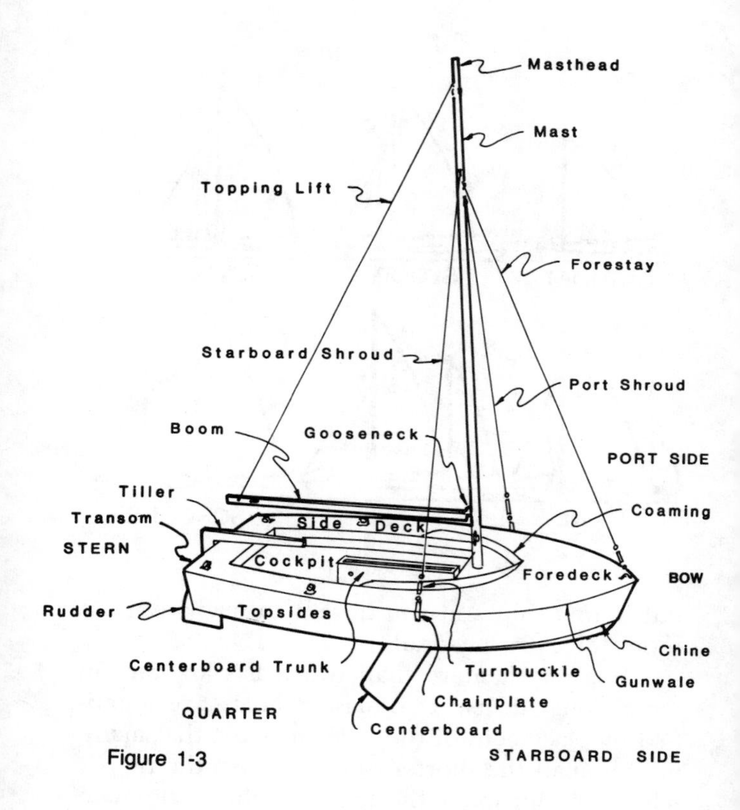

Figure 1-3

engine is classified as a power, rather than sail, vessel. How do you know if a vessel with its sails up is a powerboat? If exhaust emissions do not show, flapping sails on a steadily moving craft are a dead giveaway. A vessel 12 meters or longer, under sail and power, is required to display a black cone pointed down, but try to make sure some other way as the cone may be obscured.

The rigging of a sailing vessel may have some bearing on its maneuverability. Rigs are identified by the number and placement of their masts (fig. 1–4). A single mast near the bow of the craft identifies a catboat. Move the mast aft about a third of the boat's length and the vessel is sloop-rigged.

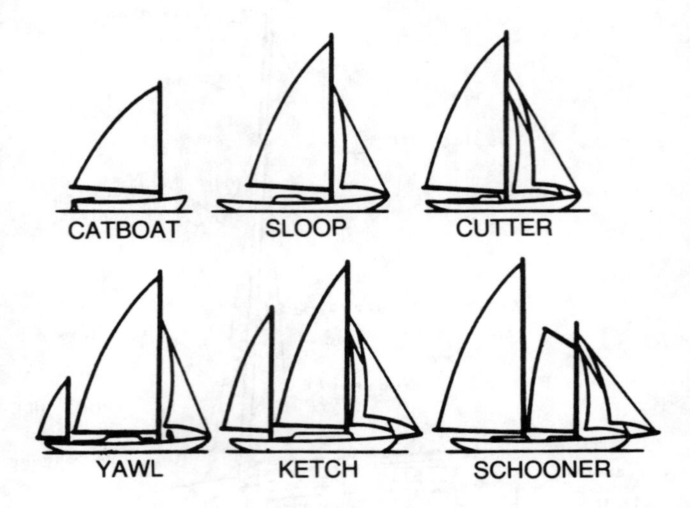

Figure 1-4

Put it amidship and you have a cutter with more room for extra headsails.

Boats with more than two masts are rare in recreational fleets. Two-masted boats are identified by placement of the taller mast. If that mainmast is abaft the shorter (the foremost) the rig is a schooner. But move the shorter behind the main and it can mark either a ketch or a yawl. It's a ketch unless the aftermast (called the mizzen) is aft of the rudder post. Then it's a yawl rig.

Motor-driven craft are not so readily packaged. Runabouts and utility boats may be driven slowly by small outboards, or at high speeds by large inboard engines. Add a deckhouse with interior accommodations and presto! you have a sedan cruiser. Wheelhouse and deck treatments vary widely on raised-deck or flush-deck cruisers. At one extreme is the flush-deck cruiser, usually larger than 40 feet, with a main deck that carries from stem to stern and a relatively unbroken sheer line from the side. At the opposite extreme is the trawler, which is bluff-bowed and has the look of a commercial fishing boat. The best motor-driven craft are moderate-speed, long-range, diesel-powered cruising boats with comfortable living quarters and sea-kindly hulls.

HULL TYPES

There is more to any boat than rig or power classification. Hull shape is basic and critical (fig. 1–6). It affects stability, speed and, sea-kindliness—all essential to seaworthiness.

The two basic types of hulls are planing (flat) and displacement (deep and rounded). Planing hulls are fast, roughriding, and less stable. Displacement hulls plow through the water and are limited to low speeds but they are quite stable. The theoretical hull speed of such a boat has been found to be related to waterline length; the longer the waterline, the greater the potential hull speed.

You can apply this mathematical relationship to your displacement hull. Maximum hull speed is approximately 1.34 times the square root of the boat's load waterline (LWL) length—that is, length with designed load aboard (fig. 1–5). For example, a boat with a waterline length of 25 feet would have a theoretical hull speed of 6.7 knots ($1.34 \times 5 = 6.7$). A boat with a 36-foot waterline would be capable of making 8.0 knots ($1.34 \times 6 = 8.0$).

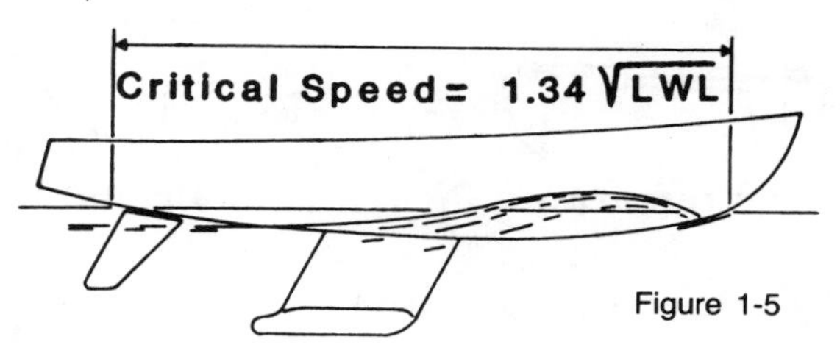

Figure 1-5

DESIGN

Boat designers strive to combine the best points of both displacement and planing hulls. Thus many powerboats act like displacement vessels at low speeds but can plane at high speeds. That compromise involves putting vee sections forward and flat sections aft to make powered craft fast enough for sportfishing and stable enough to go out where the prize fish are. Other hulls types are deep-vee, cathedral, and catamaran and are illustrated in figure 1–6. The latter two minimize drag and have excellent lateral stability. Except for certain dinghy models and multihulls, sailboats almost always are of the displacement kind.

Design is dictated by the use a boat will be put to. The sportfisherman needs a large working cockpit, high speed, and comfort offshore. Family vacationing may require the roominess and sta-

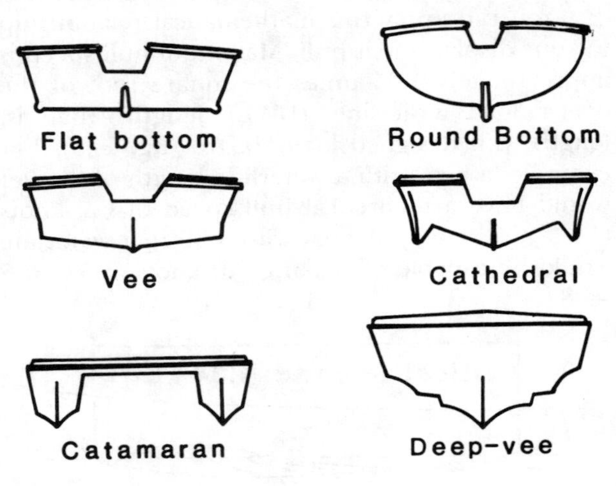

Figure 1-6

bility of a houseboat. Motor sailors give up sailing purity for roominess. And racing boats are designed for speed rather than comfort.

MATERIALS

Boats are made of any material that will stand up to the elements. Nature's boat, the floating log, undoubtedly was first. The hollowed log followed and, later, the sheathed frame. A modern boat frame may be of wood or metal and sheathed with animal hide, fabric, wood, steel, aluminum, or cement. But most boats today are made out of "fiberglass," a petroleum-based plastic reinforced by glass fibers—woven mat or chopped.

FLOTATION

Most modern boats sink when filled with water. That raises a safety question regarding flotation: Can a swamped boat float with its passengers still aboard? The Coast Guard says all boats up to 20 feet long must have buoyant material installed in their hulls that will not only keep them afloat but upright as well.

To accomplish this, voids within the boat are filled with light foam material that displaces enough water to offset the weight of the passengers and an outboard motor. This displacement material must be high in the boat so the boat will right itself if it capsizes.

CAPACITY

The number of people who can be carried safely in a boat is not determined by the number of seats. Capacity depends on hull volume, material, and design. Every boat under 20 feet long manufactured in recent years has a metal plate specifying capacity (see page 227 for Canadian Laws and Regulations).

Section 1: STUDY QUESTIONS FOR BOATING TERMS AND BOAT TYPES

1. A friend was telling about his new boat. It is a 32-foot sportfisherman. You could visualize it as:

   (a) having a high bluff bow, a broad stern, and substantial deckhouse.
   (b) rather slow, with a high bow and a large deckhouse.
   (c) probably having two outboard motors.
   (d) having a large cockpit and fairly fast.

2. On Sunday night at the marina, two friends were arguing about a sailboat docked nearby. You saw that it had two masts with the forward mast a little shorter than the after mast. It was a:

   (a) ketch.
   (b) schooner.
   (c) cutter.
   (d) yawl.

3. If a sloop is compared with a motorsailer of the same length:

   (a) the sloop is slower than the motorsailer under sail.
   (b) the motorsailer always has two or more masts.
   (c) the cabin of the sloop is usually smaller and more crowded.
   (d) the motorsailer is built for racing.

4. A sailboat with two forward sails (jibs) may be a:

   (a) ketch.
   (b) yawl.
   (c) cutter.
   (d) any of these.

5. Which of the following does not characterize a catboat? It:

   (a) has the mast well forward, in the bow.
   (b) has one marconi-rigged sail.
   (c) has three sails.
   (d) is a popular small sailboat.

6. A flush-deck cruiser:

   (a) always has a large cockpit.
   (b) is generally longer than 40 feet.
   (c) has a flying bridge.
   (d) has an enclosed wheelhouse well forward.

7. Houseboats are popular on inland lakes and rivers because:

   (a) they are easy to control in the wind.
   (b) they have fast displacement hulls.
   (c) they have large living quarters.
   (d) all of the above.

8. Most recreational boats today are built of:

   (a) wood.
   (b) ferrocement.
   (c) aluminum.
   (d) plastic (fiberglass).

9. Runabouts may have:

   (a) a large cabin.
   (b) a fishing tower.
   (c) outboard, inboard, or I/O power.
   (d) one mast.

10. Displacement hulls:

   (a) go faster with increased horsepower.
   (b) pound severely in rough water.
   (c) plow through the water and have a limited speed.
   (d) have flat bottoms.

11. A 32-foot sailboat with a displacement hull has a 25 foot load waterline (LWL) length. The maximum speed of this boat will be:

 (a) 5.2 knots.
 (b) 5.7 knots.
 (c) 6.7 knots.
 (d) 7.6 knots.

12. An advantage of a cathedral hull is:

 (a) a smoother ride than a deep-vee.
 (b) good lateral stability.
 (c) smaller wetted surface than other hull types.
 (d) all the above.

13. All boats less than 20 feet long, except sailboats and some special types, must have buoyant material installed sufficient to:

 (a) float upright when filled with water.
 (b) support the boat, motor, and crew.
 (c) both a and b.
 (d) none of the above.

14. The safe load for a boat, in persons, depends on:

 (a) the space in the cockpit.
 (b) the number of seats.
 (c) hull volume, material, and design.
 (d) the size of the engine.

15. The major structural member in a powerboat is the:

 (a) flying bridge.
 (b) transom.
 (c) super-structure.
 (d) keel.

16. The width of a boat is denoted by the:

 (a) beam.
 (b) sheer.
 (c) tumblehome.
 (d) flare.

17. The keel on a sailboat provides the boat with:

    (a) resistance to side slip.
    (b) a counterweight or ballast for stability.
    (c) better steering ability.
    (d) all the above.

18. Sailboats are steered with the:

    (a) keel.
    (b) mast.
    (c) tiller.
    (d) boom.

19. Shrouds and stays on sailboats have tension applied with:

    (a) the topping lift.
    (b) turnbuckles.
    (c) chainplates.
    (d) tangs.

SECTION 2

Regulations, Safe Boating, Marlinspike, and Weather

Soon after acquiring a boat you will realize that you are now subject to a large number of unfamiliar federal and state laws and regulations. You and your boat are under the jurisdiction of hitherto unnoticed enforcement officers, such as the U.S. Coast Guard and state marine police, and you might at any moment incur a penalty for doing or failing to do things that are a mystery to you. Fortunately for you, the men and women at the front line of enforcement can be helpful: They know that the new boater cannot always digest everything all at once. But there are some basic requirements you need to be aware of before you head for open water.

GOVERNMENT REGULATIONS

REGISTERING YOUR BOAT

The Federal Boat Safety Act of 1971 permits states to assign numbers and issue certificates. If a state chooses not to do so, boats in the state are registered by the Coast Guard.

The act requires the numbering of all vessels used on waters under federal jurisdiction, and on the high seas where owned by the United States.

It applies, with rare exceptions, to all vessels equipped with propulsion machinery, regardless of horsepower. However, some states require vessels without propulsion, such as sailboats, to be registered and display numbers.

The Certificate of Number has two parts: The first two-letter symbol identifies the state of principal use; the second part is a combination of numbers and letters for individual identification.

Numbers must (a) provide good contrast with their background; (b) be at least 3 inches tall; and (c) be in block letters, painted on or attached to both sides of the forward half of the vessel where clearly visible. Also, there must be either a space or a hyphen before and after the block of numerals to set them off from the letters preceding and following them.

The registration certificate must be on board when the boat is in use and is a helpful reference for the length and hence the equipment requirements (see page 227 for Canadian Laws and Regulations).

There is another process called "documentation" which registers the boat with the Coast Guard and skips state numbering. But the Coast Guard does not promote it and some states now require registration for documented boats, so documentation, although of value to large boats, may be on the way out.

Having complied with registration, the skipper can turn to equipping his boat.

REQUIRED AND RECOMMENDED EQUIPMENT

Equipment is of two kinds: that which is required by the Federal Boat Safety Act of 1971 and additional items essential or highly recommended for safe boating. You must have those items that are specified by law, but it would be foolhardy to go out with those alone. You would be well ad-

TABLE 1

MINIMUM REQUIRED SAFETY EQUIPMENT

EQUIPMENT	CLASS A Less Than 16 Feet (4.9m)	CLASS 1 16 Feet to Less Than 26 Feet (4.9–7.9m)	EQUIPMENT	CLASS 2 26 Feet to Less Than 40 Feet (7.9-12.2m)	CLASS 3 40 Feet to Less Than 65 Feet (12.2–19.8m)
Life Preservers	One Type I, II, III, or IV for each person.	One Type I, II, or III for each person on board or being towed on water skiis, etc., plus one Type IV available to be thrown.	Life Preservers	One Type I, II, or III for each person on board or being towed on water skiis, etc., plus one Type IV available to be thrown.	
Fire extinguishers			Fire extinguishers		
When no fixed fire extinguishing system is installed in machinery space(s)	At least one B-I type approved hand portable fire extinguisher. Not required on outboard motorboats less than 26 feet (7.9m) in length and not carrying passengers for hire if the construction of such motorboats will not permit the entrapment of flammable gases or vapors.		When no fixed fire extinguishing system is installed in machinery space(s)	At least two B-I type approved hand portable fire extinguishers, or at least one B-II type approved hand portable fire extinguisher.	At least three B-I type approved hand portable fire extinguishers, or at least one B-I type plus one B-II type approved hand portable fire extinghisher.
When fixed fire extinguishing system is installed in machinery space(s)	None		When fixed fire extinguishing system is installed in machinery space(s)	At least one B-I type approved hand portable fire extinguisher.	At least two B-I type approved hand portable fire extinguishers, or at least one B-II approved unit.
Ventilation	At least two ventilator ducts fitted with cowls or their equivalent for the purpose of properly and efficiently ventilating the bilges of every engine and fuel tank compartment of boats constructed or decked over after 25 April 1940, using gasoline or other fuel having a flashpoint less than 110°F. (43°C). Boats built after 31 July 1981 must have operable power blowers.		Ventilation	At least two ventilator ducts fitted with cowls or their equivalent for the purpose of properly and efficiently ventilating the bilges of every engine and fuel tank compartment of boats constructed or decked over after 25 April 1940, using gasoline or other fuel having a flashpoint less than 110°F. (43°C). Boats built after 31 July 1981 must have operable power blowers.	
Whistle	Boats up to 39 ft. 4 in. (12m) – any device capable of making an "efficient nd sound signal" audible ½ mile.		Whistle	Boats up to 39 ft. 4 in. (12m) – any device capable of making an "efficient sound signal" audible ½ mile.	Boats 39 ft. 4 in. to 65 ft. 7 in. (12-20m) – device meeting technical specifications of Inland Rules Annex III, audible ½ mile.
Bell	Boats up to 39 ft. 4 in. (12m) – any device capable of making an "efficient sound signal."		Bell	Boats up to 39 ft. 4 in. (12m) – any device capable of making an "efficient sound signal."	Boats 39 ft. 4 in. to 65 ft. 7 in. (12-20m) – bell meeting technical specifications of Inland Rules Annex II: mouth diameter of at least 7.9 inches (200mm).
Backfire flame arrester	One approved device on each carburetor of all gasoline engines installed after 25 April 1940, except outboard motors.		Backfire flame arrester	One approved device on each carburetor of all gasoline engines installed after 25 April 1940, except outboard motors.	
Visual distress signals Required in coastal waters only.	Required only when operating at night or carrying six or fewer passengers for hire. Same equipment as for larger boats.	Orange flag with black square-and-disc (D); and an S-O-S electric light (N); or three orange smoke signals, hand held or floating (D); or three red flares of handheld, meteor, or parachute type (D/N).	Visual distress signals Required in coastal waters only.	Orange flag with black square-and-disc (D); and an S-O-S electric light (N); or three orange smoke signals, hand held or floating (D); or three red flares of handheld, meteor, or parachute type (D/N).	

The operator is responsible for the presence of required equipment in a rented craft.

vised to seek out the local Coast Guard Auxiliary member who makes courtesy checks of equipment and have him go over your boat. If you have what a prudent skipper should, he will give you an inspection decal for your boat that usually wards off needless future inspections. If something is lacking he may have good advice on where to shop for it.

In Table 1, you will see the equipment required by law. Boats are divided into size classes for equipment requirements. Bigger boats generally need more and larger equipment.

Life Preservers

One wearable life preserver (Personal Flotation Device or PFD) is required on all boats for each person aboard and several types are acceptable.

The Off-Shore Life Jacket (Type I) and the Near-Shore Life Vest (Type II) both support a person upright in water and will turn most bodies faceup that are facing downward. They differ in buoyancy: Type I buoys 22 pounds, Type II, 15 1/2 pounds. Type III, The Flotation Aid, buoys 15 1/2 pounds but lacks the turnover feature. Type I is less comfortable to wear than the others. Note that if you tow a skier, you must have a PFD for him when he comes aboard. The last, Type IV, is a device to be thrown in a man-overboard emergency. It is designed to be held on to, not worn; it must have 16 1/2 pounds of buoyancy, and does not satisfy the requirement for wearable life preservers.

Fire Extinguishers

These are another required safety item, classified by contents, size, and use. Contents may be dry chemicals, carbon dioxide, vapor (Halon), or foam. The extinguishers are marked A, B, or C for the type of fire each is best suited to quench: A for wood, paper, etc.; B for oil and gasoline; C for electrical. Extinguishers are also categorized by size ranging from Roman numeral I (the smallest) through V. I and II are portable, III is semiportable, and IV and V are too large or inconvenient to be of interest to the recreational boater. All extinguishers for on-board use must have U.S. Coast Guard approval which you will find indicated on the label.

The B type, or dry-chemical, extinguisher is the most widely used. One subtype, Halon, is particularly effective on engine room fires. It is colorless, odorless, five times heavier than air, and it leaves no residue. In tests, Halon extinguished flames in an enclosed space in less than two seconds, even with the exhaust blower operating.

Table 1 indicates the other on-board requirements.

Not Required but Needed

The list of things not required but important to have aboard can go on and on as personal tastes are exercised. But there are some basics which everyone will want to have. For instance:

Anchor and anchor line, visual distress signals (for boats where they are not officially required), compass, bilge pump, lines, fenders, radio telephone, spare prop, engine parts kit, boathook, tools, chart and charting kit, spotlight, one day's supply of food and water, radio receiver with direction finder, notebook for ship's log. A few overnight cruises will extend that list.

OTHER REGULATIONS

Several other federal regulations apply to the recreational boater:

Termination of Use Act

This act grants the Coast Guard authority to board a boat at any time. A boat operator must follow the direction of a Coast Guard Boarding Officer to take immediate and reasonable steps necessary for the safety of those aboard the vessel. These steps may include direction to (a) correct the unsafe condition immediately; (b) proceed to a mooring, dock, or anchorage; or (c) suspend further use of the boat until the condition is corrected.

For the purpose of the act, "unsafe condition" includes (a) improper navigation lights; (b) fuel leakage; (c) accumulation of fuel in the bilge or other compartment; (d) not meeting ventilation requirements for tanks and engine spaces; and (e) inadequate backfire flame control.

The Federal Boat Safety Act

This allows the states to have additional equipment requirements "if needed to meet uniquely hazardous conditions or circumstances," and many states have such requirements. Navigation lights are part of the legally required equipment, and will be discussed under "Navigational Rules."

The Federal Water Pollution Control Act of 1972

This act deals with water pollution by oil, hazardous substances, and sewage. A person who fails to notify the appropriate federal agency of a discharge can be fined up to ten thousand dollars or serve a year in jail, or both. Moreover, violators are subject to a penalty of up to five thousand dollars against the vessel owner for every discharge, reported or not, of a "harmful quantity of oil." This is defined as an amount that causes a film or sheen, or discoloration, on the surface of the water.

An Oil Discharge Prohibited placard, at least five by eight inches and made of durable material, must be placed in the machinery space of vessels, 26 feet or over.

The Boat Safety Act of 1971

This act specifies that the operator of a boat involved in a collision, accident, or other casualty, must report the incident if it results in death, injury requiring medical attention, disappearance of a person, or property damage over five hundred dollars.

When a death or disappearance occurs, notify authorities immediately. If a person disappears from a vessel under circumstances indicating death or is seriously injured, the written report must be filed within forty-eight hours. In all other cases, make a report within ten days.

If the state has no boating law requiring such reports, the report must be made to the nearest Coast Guard officer in charge.

SAFE BOATING

RESPONSIBILITY

Until you get used to it, it may be unnerving to realize that the person responsible for conforming with all the laws, rules, and regulations is you—the operator of the boat. If there's one PFD too few, who's on the carpet? Wrong-type fire extinguishers? After a while you'll make a list and check. Then you can relax.

ALCOHOL AFLOAT

Alcohol, even in small amounts, adversely affects vision, coordination, and balance; it impairs awareness and judgment, and it increases the tendency to take risks. In a survey by the National Transportation Safety Board, 70 percent of recreational boating fatalities were alcohol-related. At least one third of the boat operators involved in fatal accidents may have been intoxicated according to legal standards.

Operating Under the Influence of Alcohol

Because of the many alcohol-related boating accidents, several states have enacted *Operating Under the Influence* laws. Typically, a blood-alcohol concentration of .10 percent or more constitutes being legally intoxicated. Operators determined to be operating their vessels under the influence are frequently escorted to shore and law enforcement officials take command of the vessel.

In 1988, the Coast Guard started to enforce a set of federal regulations in states not having a drunk boating law. These regulations include the following:

Set a legal level of intoxication at .10 percent blood-alcohol content (BAC).

Allow an officer to make a determination of intoxication based on observation of the skipper's behavior.

Refusal to submit to a toxicological test—breath, urine, or blood—is automatically presumption of intoxication.

Provide a penalty of up to a thousand-dollar fine. (More stringent regulations and penalties apply to commercial operators.)

An important clarification is that the vessel must be *under way* when the skipper is observed violating the law. Anyone at anchor or at dock cannot be violating the law. The regulations provide that a Coast Guard officer may require an alcohol-breath test or make an arrest based on *observed behavior,* which includes the skipper's speech, coordination, and appearance. One of the best rules is an old one: Don't break out the bottle until the anchor is down, the sails are furled, the boat is shipshape, and there is fair weather ahead.

USING GOOD JUDGMENT

Good judgment should err on the side of safety. Better to make a wide sweep around a swimmer or diver even if he happens to be in a forbidden area rather than risk injuring him by passing too close. Keep clear of diving operations because divers can stray from the diving vessel. Respect the "Divers Down" flag on a diving buoy or a boat flying the International Code Flag A (Alpha) which signals that the boat is engaged in diving operations, is restricted in maneuverability, and has right of way. Keep a good eye on the errant jet skiers or sailboarders and give them a wide berth as even they cannot always predict their actions. The waterways are increasingly crowded. Be alert at all times when you are under way.

Whenever you leave on a cruise, you should leave behind a float plan—the itinerary you intend to follow. Leave the plan with a friend, relative, or your yacht club. Make certain to notify the float-plan holder of any changes in your plans. If you do not return as scheduled, the float plan ensures that a sensible search can be undertaken immediately.

Common courtesy usually coincides with good judgment. Your wake is your responsibility and so is any damage it does to other boats, people, or the shore. Zooming through a crowded harbor at high speed is definitely reckless, as is running too close to swimmers, other boats, or docks.

SWAMPING OR CAPSIZING

If your boat swamps (fills with water) or capsizes (turns over), you must *stay with the boat;* the shore is always farther away than it seems.

Sailboats, particularly small ones, are more liable to capsize than motorboats are, as they can be caught by an unexpected wind shift or gust.

When the wind overwhelms a boat, it can heel (tip) excessively. This causes the boat to become less controllable. Depending on the design of the boat, the rudder may come out of the water, causing a loss of steering. If you are alert and promptly ease the sheets (lines that trim the sails), the wind that caused excessive heeling will spill out of the sails and the boat will return to an upright position with no harm done. Then you can retrim the sails and continue on course.

But you must accomplish the foregoing procedure immediately. Otherwise, the boat will not right but will continue to slow and heel, and may capsize.

If you do capsize, your first step is to see that the crew is not injured and make certain everyone stays with the boat.

The second step is to right the boat: Lower the centerboard as far as it will go and get a member of the crew—the heaviest one if possible—to stand on the centerboard while holding on to the boat. This will generally prevent the boat from continuing to roll over, or "turn turtle." In that case, the mast would point downward if the water is deep enough, or perhaps be damaged by hitting the bottom.

The third step is to make sure all the lines that control sail trim are free to run. (A fouled line may have caused the predicament.)

Most often just the force of the weight on the centerboard will cause the boat to right. A young, agile skipper may be able to step onto the centerboard or keel as it comes out of the water, force the boat back to the vertical, and return to the cockpit with nothing more than wet deck shoes.

If the boat will not right, however, you may need to lower the sails to keep them from counteracting the righting force of the weight on the centerboard. Then head the bow of the boat into the wind. Again have a crew member apply weight to the centerboard. Now the boat should right, coming up bow-to-wind with equal wind pressure on both sides.

After you right the boat, some water will usually be left in the hull. You must remove this water or its weight will adversely affect trim.

WATER SKIING

Water skiing is a popular sport. Water skiing laws vary, so be sure to learn the laws in effect where you plan to ski. People being towed on skis are required to wear a Coast Guard approved life jacket. To provide communication between the tow boat and skier, the American Water Ski Association has developed a recommended set of hand signals which you should learn before you begin.

Section 2: STUDY QUESTIONS FOR REGULATIONS AND SAFE BOATING

1. Your boat is yellow with a light blue deck. After registering it and getting an assigned number, you return to the dealer and buy:
   (a) light gray plastic numbers because your spouse likes this color.
   (b) 3-inch-high block letters and numerals for both sides of the hull in a contrasting color.
   (c) a black plastic plate, 2 inches wide, with engraved numerals on it.
   (d) 3-inch-high black script numbers and letters.

2. The list of equipment the law requires to be aboard a vessel:
   (a) is all that will be needed for the safe operation of the vessel.
   (b) is insufficient for the safe and comfortable operation of the vessel.
   (c) includes navigational equipment such as compass, charts, etc.
   (d) does not include sound signaling devices.

3. Federal Regulations require that a 15-foot boat have aboard:
   (a) one Life Preserver for each person aboard.
   (b) an anchor and sufficient line to securely anchor in that body of water in which the craft normally operates.
   (c) a compass, charts, mooring lines, and fenders.
   (d) a radiotelephone.

4. The life preserver designed for open, rough, remote waters and will turn most unconscious wearers face up in the water is the:
   (a) special use device.
   (b) flotation aid.
   (c) near-shore life vest.
   (d) off-shore life jacket.

5. Responsibility to have all legally required equipment on a rented boat is that of:

   (a) the owner.
   (b) the operator.
   (c) both owner and operator.
   (d) the manufacturer of the boat.

6. Groups into which boats are divided by Federal Regulations pertaining to certain required equipment are:

   (a) up to 16 feet and over 16 feet but less than 24 feet.
   (b) up to 26 feet and over 26 feet but less than 60 feet.
   (c) less than 16 feet, 16 feet to less than 26 feet, 26 feet to less than 40 feet, 40 feet to 65 feet.
   (d) less than 16 feet, 16 feet and over.

7. A fire extinguisher with the type classification "A" is for use on:

   (a) an electrical fire.
   (b) a gasoline fire.
   (c) a wood fire.
   (d) all of the above.

8. When using a dry chemical fire extinguisher, you should know that it:

   (a) need not be refilled if the pressure gauge indicates sufficient pressure still remains in the bottle.
   (b) is not very effective for fires in a cabin, paint locker, or other above-deck space.
   (c) must be directed on the base of the fire thereby cutting off the oxygen necessary for the flame.
   (d) both a and b above.

9. The Halon extinguishant:
   (a) is odorless, colorless, and 5 times heavier than air.
   (b) is of the same type for both portable and built-in extinguishers.
   (c) leaves a powdery residue.
   (d) all of the above.

10. Visual Distress Signal Devices carried aboard a powered 16-foot vessel:
   (a) must be on board at all times.
   (b) must be useful in daylight.
   (c) must be useful at night.
   (d) all of the above.

11. The law relating to equipment requires that a vessel be equipped with:
   (a) a flame arrestor if it has an inboard gasoline engine.
   (b) a proper ventilation system if it has enclosed engine or fuel tank compartments.
   (c) sound signaling equipment.
   (d) all of the above.

12. Ventilation systems must be:
   (a) capable of keeping cabin air fresh.
   (b) capable of ducting fresh air into engine and fuel tank compartments.
   (c) capable of keeping bilges dry.
   (d) Coast Guard approved.

13. For the purposes of the "Termination of Use" act, an unsafe condition exists when:
   (a) a vessel is not maneuverable.
   (b) a vessel needs a tow to the nearest harbor.
   (c) a vessel does not display the navigational lights prescribed between sunset and sunrise.
   (d) all of the above.

14. A Coast Guard Boarding Officer may order the operator to:

    (a) correct an especially hazardous condition immediately.
    (b) proceed to a mooring, dock, or anchorage.
    (c) suspend further use of the boat until the especially hazardous condition is corrected.
    (d) all of the above.

15. The Federal Water Pollution Control Act of 1972 requires:

    (a) a person to notify the appropriate Federal Agency of an oil, hazardous substances, and/or sewage spill or discharge.
    (b) a placard entitled "Discharge of Oil Prohibited" be placed in the machinery space of every vessel 26 feet or over.
    (c) assessment of a fine against both the person who fails to notify the appropriate Federal Agency of a pollution discharge and the owner of the offending vessel.
    (d) all of the above.

16. Your 20-foot I/O boat has a center console steering station. The seats just ahead of the engine are a little noisy and your guest doesn't like to sit there, but prefers the forward "bowrider" seat. The two children always want to ride on the bow deck with their feet hanging over. As skipper you know that:

    (a) you should never let anyone sit on the bow of a small powerboat.
    (b) excessive weight forward increases drag, reduces speed, and makes steering difficult.
    (c) your passengers should be seated where they will not appreciably affect the level trim of the boat.
    (d) all of the above.

17. The law requires that if death occurs within 24 hours of an accident, or a person disappears from a vessel under circumstances indicating death or injury, the report must be made:

    (a) within 48 hours.
    (b) within 10 days.
    (c) to the nearest police department.
    (d) as soon as possible.

18. If your boat swamps or capsizes:

    (a) have one crew member swim to shore for help.
    (b) everyone should swim for shore, but stay together.
    (c) stay with the boat.
    (d) none of the above.

19. When fueling an outboard with portable tanks, you should:

    (a) fill the tank to the top so as not to run out of gas.
    (b) put the tank on the dock to fill it.
    (c) put the tank on a seat to fill it.
    (d) use a plastic funnel to prevent spilling any gas.

20. Alcohol is related to recreational boating accidents in:

    (a) from 25 to 30 percent of cases involving fatalities.
    (b) more than 65 percent of cases involving fatalities.
    (c) less than 15 percent of accidents.
    (d) less than 25 percent of accidents.

21. A puff of wind has caused your sailboat to heel severely and you don't want to capsize. Your first reaction should be to:

    (a) fall off the wind.
    (b) ease the main and jib until the boat stabilizes.
    (c) turn dead downwind.
    (d) push the centerboard down to counteract the heeling.

22. Your boat has just capsized. Your first step should be to:

(a) look around for outside assistance.
(b) get some weight on the centerboard.
(c) get the sails down.
(d) check to be sure that all crew are OK.

23. The reason you want your sailboat headed into the wind when you try to right it after a capsize is to:

(a) have the boat headed in the correct direction.
(b) have equal pressure on both sides of the sails as the boat comes up.
(c) make it easier for the rescue boat to throw a line downwind to you.
(d) permit the sails to be lowered more readily.

24. If a law enforcement officer, through observation, suspects a boater is intoxicated, federal drunk boating law regulations provide that the officer can:

(a) require the boater to take an alcohol breath test.
(b) impose a fine of up to $1,000.
(c) require all aboard to put on life jackets.
(d) all of the above.

25. As you are cruising across a lake, you notice several board-sailers approaching from your right. As a safety precaution, you should:

(a) speed up so you pass in front of them.
(b) continue your course because you have the right-of-way.
(c) continue surveillance and if necessary, change course to give them a wide berth.
(d) slow down so they will pass in front of you.

26. Water ski hand signals are designed to provide a means of communication between the:
    (a) skier and other boaters on the water.
    (b) skier and the tow boat.
    (c) tow boat and other boaters in the area.
    (d) skier and other recreational water sports enthusiasts such as boardsailers and jet skiers.

27. You decide to purchase new life jackets. Your boating is done on inland lakes and rivers. The appropriate type of life preserver for this use will be:
    (a) an offshore jacket because you can go anywhere with these and they are the best one can buy.
    (b) a throwable device since you will never be far from shore.
    (c) a flotation aid because these will be suitable for water skiing too.
    (d) a near-shore life vest because rescue will be relatively fast.

28. Float plans are filed with:
    (a) the Coast Guard when cruising on international waters.
    (b) a friend or relative.
    (c) the local sheriff's office.
    (d) all of the above.

29. You are cruising in open water which is about 100 feet deep. You notice a boat some distance in front of you that is flying the International Code Flag "Alpha," This vessel is:
    (a) anchored and engaged in fishing.
    (b) stopped so the guests can swim from the boat.
    (c) having engine trouble and you should go over to see if you can assist or provide a tow.
    (d) engaged in diving operations, restricted in its maneuverability, and has the right-of-way.

Here are some basic terms, uses, and knots.

ROPE is the common term applied to cordage in the original coil or reel. Fiber rope is either natural fiber (manila, sisal, cotton, hemp) or synthetic fiber (nylon, Dacron,® polypropylene, etc.). Synthetic rope is so much superior in strength and characteristics that most skippers will find natural rope a false economy.

LINE is how rope is referred to when put to use aboard a boat, and each is given a specific name, such as halyard, sheet, rode, and dock line. There are exceptions when the term "rope" is included in the specific name. Among these are rope on a bell, a tiller, or a bucket; manropes (for personal safety); and boltropes.

STANDING PART is the section of the line that leads to the secured end (usually to a cleat or a bitt). It is also the portion of the line not used in making the knot, or the part of the line around which the knot may be tied. It is normally under strain.

FREE END is the section of line, not secured or under strain, that is used to form the knot.

KNOT is a general term including bends and hitches as well as "knots." Each serves best in a particular circumstance and is not suitable in

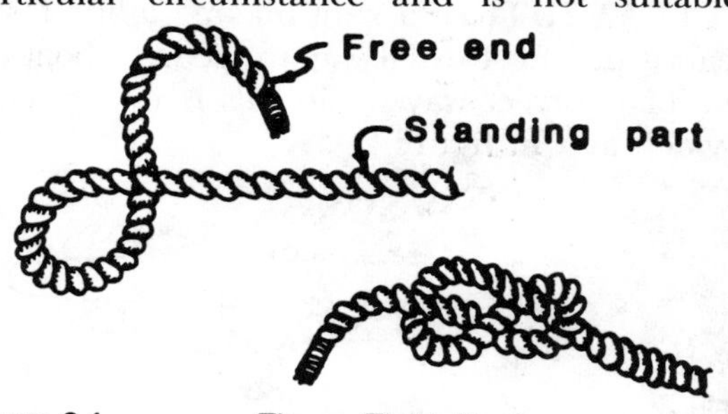

Figure 2-1 Figure-Eight Knot

other situations. There are four basic, common knots:

FIGURE-EIGHT KNOT is the basic kind of stopper knot—a knot tied in the end of a line to keep it from running out of a block, grommet, or other opening, or temporarily to keep a line from unraveling (fig. 2–1).

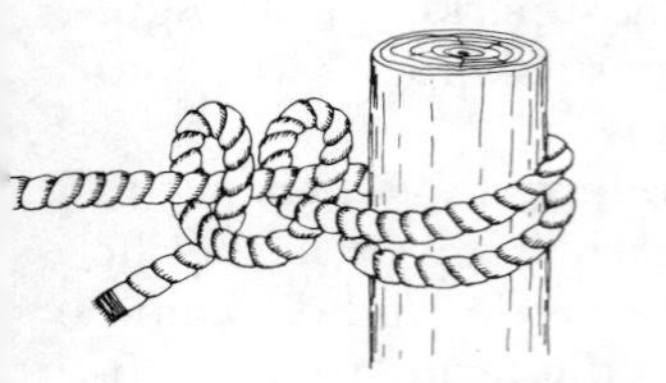

Round Turn and Two Half Hitches

Figure 2-2

ROUND TURN AND TWO HALF-HITCHES is the most useful and secure method to tie a line to a pile or post, although this can be done in a number of ways. This hitch can also be used to secure a line to a ring, spar, or post too high to pass a loop over. It is easily untied, yet can be used for a permanent tie-up.

To tie this knot, simply pass the line twice around the pile or through the ring. Then, with the free end, make two half-hitches on the standing part (fig. 2–2).

CLEAT HITCH, a knot making a line fast to a cleat, is the most usual way to secure a boat to a dock. The correct way to do this is illustrated in the video and in figure 2–3.

Figure 2-3

Cleat Hitch

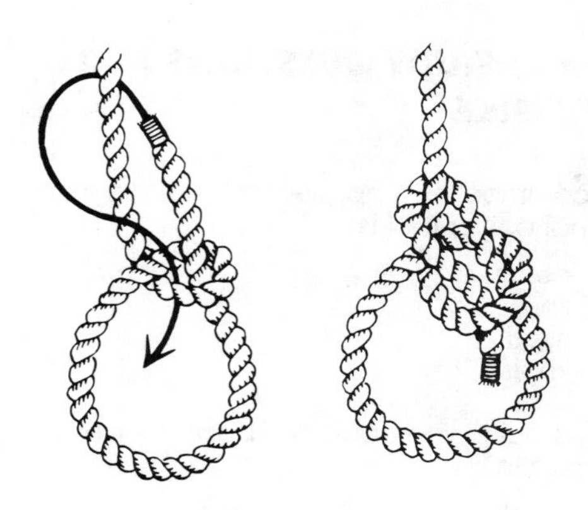

Bowline Knot

Figure 2-4

BOWLINE is probably the most important knot (fig. 2–4). It is easy to tie, will not slip or jam, is easy to untie, and is the most versatile of knots. The bowline forms a secure loop that can be placed over a cleat, pile, post, or bollard as a dock line. It can be used to tie to a mooring ring or an anchor ring. Lines large and small, equal and unequal in size, can be tied together by using a bowline in the end of each. By passing the standing part of the line through the loop, a free-running noose can be made.

To tie a bowline, first form a small loop, making sure the free end is on top of the standing part. Now take the bitter end (free end), pass it up through the loop, then pass it behind the standing part and back through the loop.

(Most the lines found aboard a sailboat—this includes dock lines, anchor rodes, halyards, spare lines [everything but the mainsheet and the jib sheets, the so-called working lines]—should be properly coiled when you are under way. For more information on how to do this and additional knots, see Chapman's, ch. 13.)

Section 2: STUDY QUESTIONS FOR MARLINSPIKE

1. The common term applied to cordage in the original coil or reel is:

   (a) cords.
   (b) line.
   (c) rope.
   (d) knots.

2. Ropes put to use aboard a boat are generally referred to as:

   (a) cords.
   (b) lines.
   (c) ropes.
   (d) knots.

3. The section of a line leading to the secured end is called:

   (a) the bitter end.
   (b) the free end.
   (c) the standing part.
   (d) the knot.

4. The best stopper knot is:

   (a) a bowline.
   (b) an overhand knot.
   (c) a round turn and two half-hitches.
   (d) a figure-eight knot.

5. The most useful method to secure a line to a pile is:

   (a) a figure-eight knot.
   (b) a round turn and two half-hitches.
   (c) several wraps around the pile.
   (d) none of the above.

6. The lines aboard a sailboat that should be properly coiled when under way are:

   (a) mainsheet and jibsheets.
   (b) spare lines and jibsheets.
   (c) dock lines, anchor rodes, and halyards.
   (d) halyards and mainsheet.

7. The most versatile and useful knot is a:

   (a) cleat hitch.
   (b) bowline.
   (c) figure-eight.
   (d) round turn and two half-hitches.

8. The bowline can be used:

   (a) to form a loop that will not jam or slip.
   (b) to make a free-running noose.
   (c) to connect two lines of different size by using a bowline in the end of each.
   (d) all the above.

9. The knot that permits good snubbing leverage when being tied, yet is easily released while under load is the:

   (a) cleat hitch.
   (b) round turn and two half-hitches.
   (c) figure-eight.
   (d) bowline.

10. A stopper knot is used to:

   (a) keep a line from running out of a block.
   (b) temporarily keep a line from unraveling.
   (c) keep a line in a grommet.
   (d) all the above.

Most people have learned about weather from watching their favorite TV weather announcer. These specialists talk of halcyon highs with clockwise winds and the stormy lows that blow in the opposite direction, of warm and cold fronts, each with its special signature of cloud type and prologue of rain or fog. Best of all, they interpret these conditions, telling what the weather will be like in a given region for the next day or so. Even more reliable is the National Weather Service's continuous broadcast of weather information that can be picked up by any marine VHF–FM transceiver. This reports the specific marine conditions, giving wind speed, wave heights, temperature dew point, and humidity so you can make your own fog prediction, and, of course, storm warnings are broadcast.

A boater should be most concerned with forecasts of lightning, fog, and the sudden squalls that are part of any boating season.

PRESSURE SYSTEMS AND FRONTS

Pressure systems, areas of high or low atmospheric pressure, control the movements of the various air masses, holding one type in one area, replacing one type with another type, or bringing about a clash of differing masses in a zone of converging wind flow. In this way the high- and low-pressure systems play a major part in determining the type of weather we are likely to have—clear, calm, windy, wet, stormy.

Low-pressure systems generate severe and hazardous weather ranging from mile-wide tornadoes to 200–400-mile-wide tropical hurricanes and even 1,000-mile-wide extratropical cyclones (lows), the major weather makers of the middle latitudes.

Figure 2-5

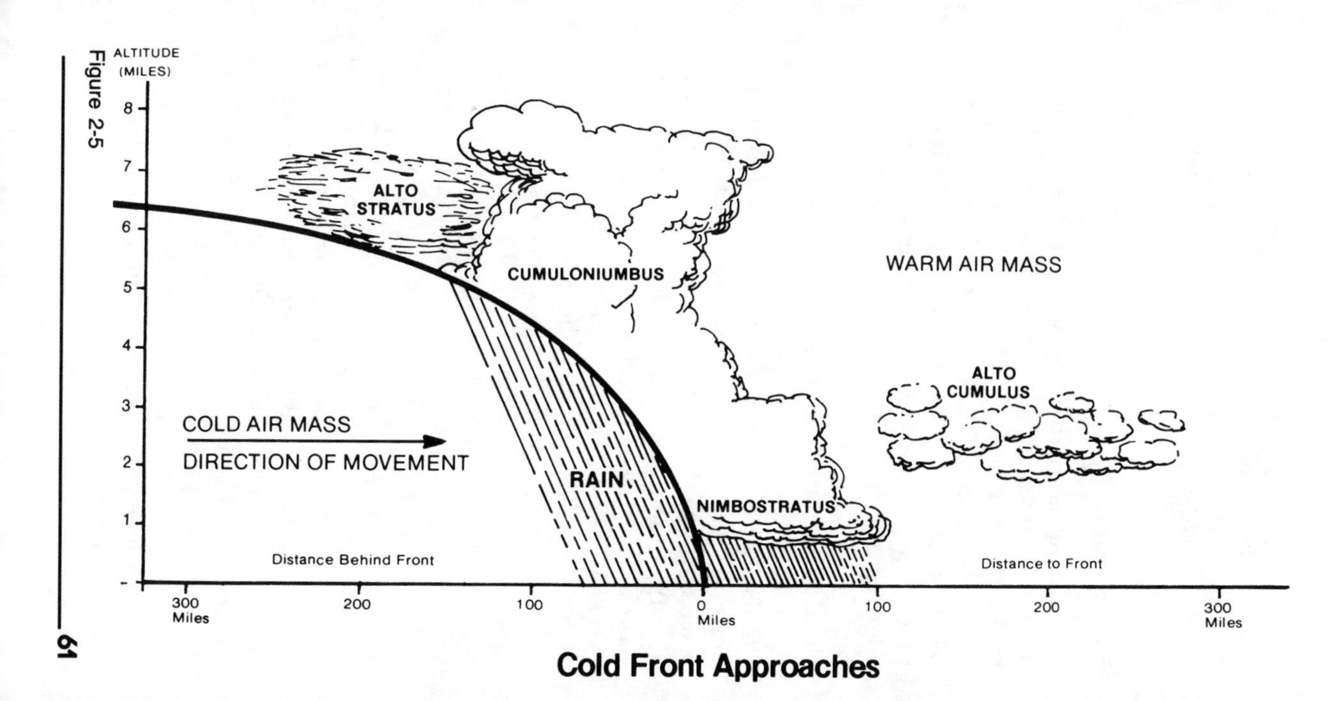

Cold Front Approaches

High-pressure systems are broad areas, usually several hundred thousand square miles of atmosphere with uniform temperature and moisture content.

Front Passage

A **front** is the boundary between two masses of air. The passage of a front results in a change in the weather.

For example, the oncoming cold air mass in a *cold front* pushes under the warm air and forces it upward (fig. 2–5). The steep slope of the leading edge causes the warm air to be pushed aloft rapidly. This rapid cooling generates cumulus clouds and thunderstorms. An approaching cold front is indicated by a wall of dark threatening clouds. The barometric pressure drops and clouds descend as the front approaches. Rain showers start slowly and increase with winds veering usually from southwest to northwest as the front passes. Skies clear quickly, the visibility becomes excellent, and the temperature drops.

A *warm front,* on the other hand, occurs when the advancing warm air mass reaches colder air and rides up over it (fig. 2–6). The slope of the warm front is not as steep as that of a cold front—about one mile in height for every hundred miles long. Warm fronts do not move as fast as cold fronts and are eventually overtaken by cold fronts. Warm-front weather is milder than cold-front weather and may extend several hundred miles in advance of the actual front. Precipitation is generally lighter, more widespread, and lasts for a longer period of time. The approach of the warm front is indicated by formation of high-altitude clouds, then gradually lowering stratus clouds. The barometer fall is more gradual than with the onset of a cold front.

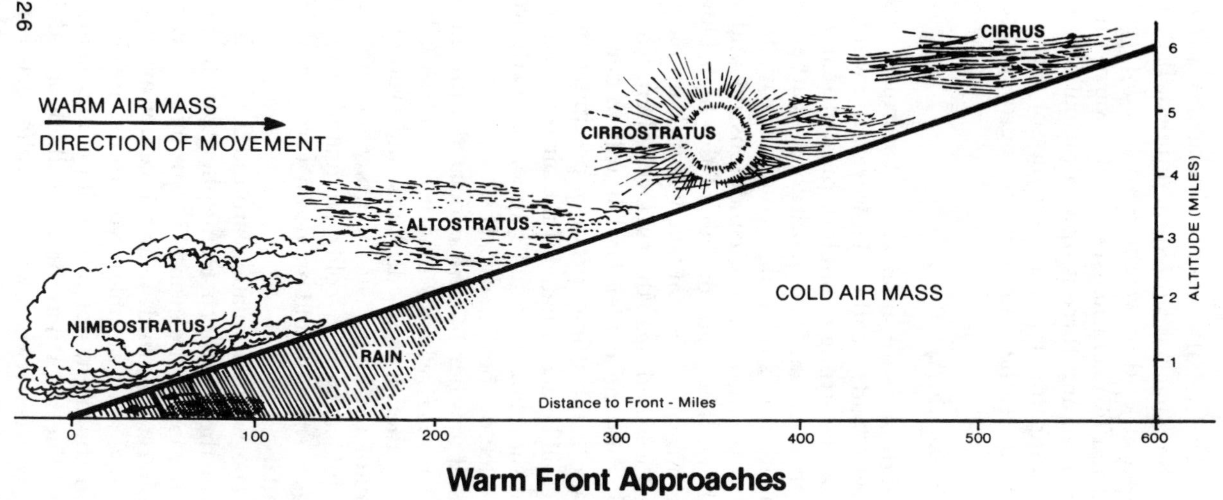

Warm Front Approaches
WARM AIR MASS
DIRECTION OF MOVEMENT
COLD AIR MASS
CIRRUS
CIRROSTRATUS
ALTOSTRATUS
NIMBOSTRATUS
RAIN
ALTITUDE (MILES)
1
2
3
4
5
6
Distance to Front - Miles
0
100
200
300
400
500
600

Figure 2-6

Other frontal conditions occur. A *stationary front* is one that has slowed or stopped. It delivers warm-front kind of weather. An *occluded front* occurs when two cold masses pinch a warm one between them and force it upward, usually as a low is breaking up. It produces a mix of warm- and cold-front weather until the fronts grow indistinct.

Anticyclone Weather

High-pressure areas are not normally associated with "bad" weather. However, the winds of a high can be strong enough to present real danger to a small boat. Such hazardous weather arises when the winds of a high combine with the *lake effect* to produce stormy conditions on and near the shore. The cold, dry air of the high blowing across a relatively warm lake will pick up moisture and be warmed near the surface. Then, when the air reaches the colder land it will undergo condensation, and it may produce precipitation. This effect will be accentuated if the air is forced to rise at the shoreline, as often happens in early winter in the lee of the Great Lakes.

Still another hazard associated with the high is the *norther,* which can cause wind squalls and cold weather in the Gulf states, and even over the waters of the Gulf. This occurs when the leading edge of a strong, cold, elongated anticyclone brings a wave of cold air down very rapidly from Canada.

The wind circulation around a high is clockwise in the Northern Hemisphere. In highs, unlike in lows, the wind is strongest near the periphery; the winds near the center are likely to be weak and variable. No fronts are involved within the high, nor any well-defined cloud patterns. The high may be a small, poorly defined area between two lows—the calm between the storms—or it may be a large, roughly circular system that can influence approaching lows.

A strong, slow-moving or stationary high will cause a following low to slow down and be deflected toward the north in the North Hemisphere. This *blocking effect* is most pronounced when a high moves eastward across the country and merges with the Bermuda high. The result is an unusually strong, large, and virtually stationary high. This will cause any low that is following its normal course toward the East Coast to slow or stop, and then to turn northward. This common summertime phenomenon often shields the Southeastern states from frontal effects for considerable periods. The somewhat similar Hawaiian high is centered near the Hawaiian Islands. This blocking high protects Southern California from almost all lows throughout the year. During the summer, the Hawaiian high intensifies and extends protection to the entire West Coast.

COMMON DANGERS

Fog. Fog occurs when moist air is cooled to its dew point—the temperature at which water vapor in the air condenses into small droplets and precipitates as a dense mist. On a clear night with a very light breeze, the cooling of the earth's surface by radiation into space will result in the formation of radiation fog. The next morning as the sun rises and warms the air a few degrees, the condensed moisture evaporates and the fog disappears. An increase in the wind will also dissipate radiation fog.

Another type of fog, called advection fog, occurs when warm moist air—previously over land or a large body of warmer water—passes over the surface of cooler water. This type of fog persists until the conditions generating it change, which may take several days. Advection fog is particu-

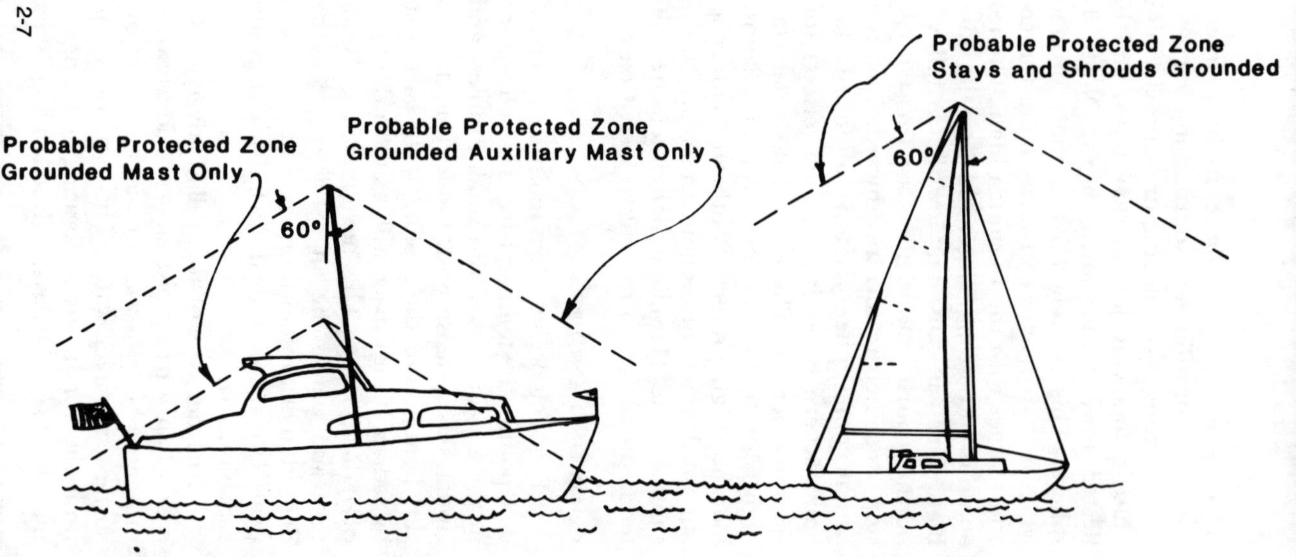
Probable Protected Zone
Grounded Mast Only
60°
Probable Protected Zone
Grounded Auxiliary Mast Only
Probable Protected Zone
Stays and Shrouds Grounded
60°

Figure 2-7

larly hazardous because it moves in a bank and can overtake and surprise you even on a relatively clear day.

Lightning. Lightning strikes small boats with disastrous results. The speed of a lightning bolt will reach 250,000 mph. The best protection is a properly grounded antenna or mast that is high enough to provide a cone of protection (an umbrella) large enough to cover the hull (fig. 2–7).

Thunderstorms. Thunderstorms generally occur when weather fronts intersect. They also result from the sun's heating of the earth. Respect either type; both hit hard.

A thunderstorm involves a pillar of cloud that may rise as high as fifty thousand feet. Its system includes very strongly gusting winds, heavy rain, reduced visibility, and rough seas.

It is distinguished by its topknot "anvil cloud" and a roller cloud near the base. Heralded by distant thunder, the black clouds move from west to east rapidly with the anvil pointing the way. The storm arrives with a hard gust of wind. Rain and more wind follow.

A thunderstorm gives some warning and you have a few minutes to prepare. If you can reach shelter in time, head for it. Other choices are to run before the storm if there is plenty of sea room, to stop and anchor, or, on a slow engine, to chug forward into the wind. Running has an advantage: Your forward speed reduces the velocity of the apparent wind.

Section 2: STUDY QUESTIONS FOR WEATHER

1. Marine weather information can be obtained from:
   (a) the National Weather Service stations.
   (b) the Coast Guard via VHF–FM marine radiotelephone.
   (c) local television and radio stations.
   (d) all the above.

2. Pressure systems and their movement are important because they:
   (a) play a major role in the type of weather that develops.
   (b) cause barometric pressure changes.
   (c) cause the wind to change directions.
   (d) create cloudiness.

3. The most severe and hazardous weather is generated by:
   (a) high pressure systems.
   (b) occluded fronts.
   (c) low pressure systems.
   (d) cold fronts.

4. The direction of wind circulation around a low in the Northern Hemisphere is:
   (a) downward.
   (b) counterclockwise.
   (c) clockwise.
   (d) no wind in a low.

5. During the day the temperature is warm and the wind is from the southwest. At night you are awakened by thunderstorms. The next morning brings clear skies, lower temperatures, and a northwest wind. You have experienced:

   (a) a warm frontal passage through the area.
   (b) a squall line passing through.
   (c) the arrival of a low pressure system.
   (d) a cold frontal passage.

6. After several days of clear weather, you notice high altitude clouds. The following day the sky is overcast and the temperature is warmer. You can expect:

   (a) thunderstorms because a cold front is coming.
   (b) a steady rain from the onset of a warm front.
   (c) clear skies within 8 hours.
   (d) strong winds to develop.

7. You are planning on a Sunday cruise. Sunday's weather forecast predicts a low will be almost 200 miles directly south of you. Your Sunday weather prediction will be:

   (a) rain all day.
   (b) clear skies.
   (c) probably cloudy, moderate wind, no rain.
   (d) a cold front passing through about noon.

8. Weather associated with an anticyclone, or a high, includes:

   (a) northerly winds bringing cold air from the arctic.
   (b) possible high winds at the periphery of the high.
   (c) the stalling or northerly diversion of easterly moving lows.
   (d) all the above.

9. Radiation fog, which often forms overnight and envelops harbors and shorelines:

(a) usually dissipates when the temperature drops.
(b) may persist for several days.
(c) usually dissipates when the temperature rises a few degrees as the sun rises.
(d) is usually a winter phenomenon.

10. A fog that moves in a bank and may quickly overtake a coastal boater is called:

(a) navigation fog.
(b) advection fog.
(c) radiation fog.
(d) convection fog.

11. Hazards associated with thunderstorms include:

(a) heavy rains.
(b) high winds.
(c) lightning.
(d) all the above.

12. Early warning of an approaching thunderstorm can come from keeping an eye on the cloud formations. The skipper should look for:

(a) low dark clouds to the west.
(b) large clouds with an anvil top moving from the east.
(c) high winds and heavy rains to the east.
(d) large clouds with an anvil top moving from the west.

13. If you see a thunderstorm approaching, the best course of action is:

(a) find a safe harbor.
(b) head into the storm to get through it quickly.
(c) ignore it since they tend to be localized and probably will not come your way.
(d) hold your position until the storm passes.

14. In order for a mast or antenna to provide a cone of protection, it must be:

(a) grounded to the water.
(b) made of metal.
(c) cylindrical in shape.
(d) a and b.
(e) all the above.

SECTION 3

Charts, Aids to Navigation, and Regional Boating

Both charts and aids to navigation are covered in detail in the video presentation but there is a little more we should tell you about buoys. Buoys are the recreational boater's closest friend afloat. He progresses from departure to destination by going from buoy to buoy, often sighting the next one ahead before the last one has disappeared behind. If they are not that close together he navigates from one to the next by dead reckoning.

A buoy does not come into sight as a clear, colored shape flaunting its number. It appears silhouetted against the horizon line like a black pencil dot. In time it emerges from the dot and takes shape but you have to get quite close before the color is clear.

The video shows the shapes, colors, lighting, and special characteristics of the floating aids. It sounds their sounds of bells, gongs, whistles, and horns. You need to know in addition a few more specialized types of navigation aids that you might encounter.

BUOYAGE SYSTEMS

A wide channel, or the entrance to a long

channel or fairway may be marked with a safe water (mid-channel) buoy painted *red* and *white* in vertical stripes. This kind of buoy is often identified with a two-letter abbreviation identifying the channel it marks.

When lighted, the safe water buoy has the same shape as other lighted buoys, appears red and white, shows a *white* light flashing a short and a long flash, (the Morse code letter *A*) and has a red spherical shape on top. A lighted safe water buoy is shown on a chart as an unshaded diamond with a vertical line with small circles at both the top and bottom, and the letters *RW* and *Mo(A)*. Your vessel should pass a safe water buoy close aboard on either side.

PREFERRED CHANNEL AIDS

An obstruction or junction in a channel may be marked by a numberless buoy painted with green and red horizontal bands and may be lighted or unlighted. When the principal channel bears off to the right, heading upstream, the unlighted buoy is *can-shaped* with the top band *green*. When lighted, the shape is similar to other buoys with the top band *green* and a green light with a Composite Group Flashing (2 + 1) sequence. This buoy is shown on charts with a diamond similar to other buoys with the top half green and the bottom half magenta and the letters *GR*. Lighted buoys are shown similarly with a magenta disk. To remain in the preferred channel these buoys should be passed to port.

When the principal channel is to the left, the unlighted buoy is a *nun*, and the topmost band is *red*. A lighted buoy for this situation is similar to the one for a preferred channel to the right except the top band is *red* and the light is red. The chart symbols are the colored diamond with the top half magenta and the bottom half green and the letters *RG*.

At such a junction, the numbers of the principal channel continue their sequence, but the numbers of the secondary channel start over with 1, 2, 3, 4, etc.

RANGES

The special use of two beacons to indicate the center line of a channel or fairway, or to point a direction for other uses, is known as a range. These beacons may vary in shape and color, particularly where one range leads to another. Further, to distinguish one from another, these ranges may be lettered rather than numbered. The front marker is lower than the rear marker so the two may be seen together in a vertical line when on the range. When off the range a horizontal separation of the two markers alerts the helmsman to steer the vessel back into the center of the channel.

Lighted ranges are much the same as day ranges. The rear marker often has a light that is on longer than the front light is. Various colors and flashing characteristics are used to help identify and differentiate the two markers. Again, keeping them in a vertical line keeps the vessel in midchannel.

Section 3: STUDY QUESTIONS FOR CHARTS AND AIDS TO NAVIGATION

1. A nautical chart is:

   (a) of little use to the pleasure boater.
   (b) concerned with only hazards to navigation.
   (c) concerned with both natural and manmade features.
   (d) none of the above.

2. Meridians of longitude are:

   (a) imaginary lines on the earth's surface running north-south.
   (b) imaginary lines on the earth's surface parallel to the equator.
   (c) used to identify your position.
   (d) both a and c.

3. Blue areas on a nautical chart indicate:

   (a) dry land.
   (b) deep, safe water.
   (c) tidal areas, bare at low water.
   (d) shallow water.

4. Useful features shown on a tidal-water chart include:

   (a) water depths at high tide.
   (b) heights of landmarks and bridge clearances at low tide.
   (c) aids to navigation.
   (d) where the fish are located.

5. Buoys may be identified by:

   (a) their shape.
   (b) their color.
   (c) their number.
   (d) all of the above.

6. Under the Lateral System, as used in U.S. waters, when returning from the sea:

   (a) you leave red buoys to your right.
   (b) you leave green buoys to your right.
   (c) you stay well clear of red and white buoys.
   (d) you leave red buoys to your left.

7. Proceeding inward from the sea:

   (a) numbers on buoys will increase.
   (b) numbers will not be used on buoys.
   (c) numbers on buoys will decrease.
   (d) numbers on buoys will indicate local hazards.

8. In U.S. waters, red buoys will be:

   (a) even numbered.
   (b) on the right when returning from seaward.
   (c) conical shaped if not lighted.
   (d) all of the above.

9. Green lighted buoys will show what color light and numbers:

   (a) red and even.
   (b) white and odd.
   (c) green and odd.
   (d) none of the above.

10. Vertical red and white stripes on a buoy indicate:

    (a) a wreck.
    (b) midchannel.
    (c) a fork in the channel.
    (d) a diverging channel.

11. The buoy known as a CAN is:

    (a) even numbered.
    (b) cylindrical in shape.
    (c) painted red.
    (d) all of the above.

12. Red and white vertically striped buoys also have unique shapes:

    (a) unlighted buoy is spherical; lighted buoy has white spherical shape on top.
    (b) unlighted buoy is cylindrical; lighted buoy has white spherical shape on top.
    (c) unlighted buoy is spherical; lighted buoy has red spherical shape on top.
    (d) unlighted buoy is conical; lighted buoy has red spherical shape on top.

13. At the junction of two channels:

    (a) the principal channel continues the buoy number sequence.
    (b) the inferior channel starts its number sequence over again from "1" and "2."
    (c) both a and b.
    (d) neither a nor b.

14. Preferred channel buoys are:

    (a) black and white.
    (b) red and green.
    (c) red and white.
    (d) green and white.

15. A lighted buoy indicating a preferred channel to port:

    (a) should be kept to starboard.
    (b) has a red light.
    (c) has a Composite Group Flashing (2 + 1) light characteristic.
    (d) all of the above.

16. Lateral System Daymarks are:

    (a) green squares and red triangles.
    (b) red squares and green triangles.
    (c) green and red circles.
    (d) octagons of different colors.

17. A short-long, or Morse "A" (Mo A) light is used to:

    (a) mark the sides of the channel.
    (b) mark the middle of a channel.
    (c) mark a bend in the channel.
    (d) mark an obstruction or junction in the channel.

18. The characteristics of a sound buoy may be:

(a) a bell.
(b) a gong.
(c) a whistle.
(d) any of the above.

19. A range:

(a) is made up of two distinctive beacons in line.
(b) indicates the centerline of a channel.
(c) measures distance to be run.
(d) both a and b.

20. You have been running in a strange channel and are unsure of your position. You find yourself close to a buoy which you can identify by characteristic and number. You should:

(a) turn on the Depth Sounder.
(b) locate that buoy on your chart.
(c) take cross bearings.
(d) check the time of high tide.

COASTAL BOATING

TIDES

All ocean levels rise and fall, usually twice a day, but only once a day in some places such as the Gulf of Mexico. This vertical fluctuation is called *tide*. The change varies from less than a foot at some places to 10, 12, or even 30 feet at others. Daily projections are given for many points in *Tide Tables*, published annually by the National Oceanic and Atmospheric Administration (NOAA).

Many newspapers and television stations give the times of high and low tide along with their weather reports.

You should be especially aware that the forecast height (given in feet or meters) is *not the depth of water* but is the height of water above or below the depth shown on the chart, which figures are generally based on Mean Low Water.

In areas where the range (the difference in depth between high and low tide) is considerable, you will probably want to be able to estimate the depth at times between high and low tides. Where there are two high and low tides daily (semidiurnal), the duration (time from high to low or low to high) is about six hours. Since the tide does not rise and fall at an even rate, you can estimate heights at intermediate times as follows:

During the *first 1/3* of the *duration,* the water level will change *1/4 of the range.*
During the *middle 1/3* of the *duration,* the water level will change *an additional 1/2 of the range.*
During the *last 1/3* of the *duration,* the water level will change *an additional 1/4 of the range.*

Note that the height does not increase or decrease equally each hour but changes faster during the middle one third of the rise or fall. More precise methods of calculation are explained in the *Tide Tables* published by NOAA.

Using *Tide Tables* and the procedure above, you can quickly convert charted depth to actual depth for any given time and place. Knowing the depth of water and your draft, you can determine whether safe passage over shoals is possible. However, not every point on a chart has been measured, so it is possible that a shoal could have formed since the last survey, or that there is a rock between the charted depths. It is prudent to allow a safety margin. Weather factors, such as hurricanes hundreds of miles away, can cause abnormal variations in height of tides. Heavy rains, extended droughts, and prolonged winds from one direction should be considered. When boating in unfamiliar waters it is a good idea to obtain local knowledge about tides, currents, shoals, or peculiar conditions along your projected course.

TIDAL CURRENTS

As the tide rises and falls, there is a horizontal movement of water termed *tidal current.* This is called flood when the flow is toward land, and ebb when the flow is toward the sea. Tidal currents, like the heights of tides, can vary significantly—from less than half a knot to six knots or more. A current of even a knot or two can make your passage faster or slower and can move you off course, possibly into dangerous areas. Here are some general rules for determining tidal current velocity.

Maximum tidal current velocity occurs during the middle third of the duration.

At high and low tide, tidal current velocity is often zero or nearly so in many places.

Tidal currents reverse direction, nearly 180 degrees in most cases, with each tidal cycle.

At the mouth of a river or in a narrow inlet, fast-running currents can be treacherous and should either be avoided or traversed with extreme caution. Rips *occur where a fast current passes over an irregular bottom or where there are sudden changes in depth, often around exposed headlands.* Tidal rips *accompany tidal changes, are often close to shore, and can be very turbulent. Navigate with caution.*

For more information on tides and currents, see Chapman's, ch. 15.

Section 3: STUDY QUESTIONS FOR COASTAL BOATING

1. The rise and fall of ocean levels is called tide. Tides are:

   (a) caused by severe storms.
   (b) uniform along a coast.
   (c) predictable.
   (d) none of the above.

2. Height of tide—published in the *Tide Tables* or newspapers, or given with weather forecasts—is:

   (a) the water depth at a given location.
   (b) the charted depth at a given location.
   (c) an exact measurement.
   (d) an adjustment that is added to or subtracted from the charted depth to obtain the water depth.

3. The tide rises and falls:

   (a) faster during the middle ⅓ of the duration.
   (b) at a uniform rate throughout the duration.
   (c) faster during the first and last ⅓ of the duration.
   (d) none of the above.

4. Tidal currents:

   (a) are predictable.
   (b) vary in velocity during the tidal cycle.
   (c) reverse direction.
   (d) all of the above.

5. Narrow inlets connect many rivers and bays to the sea. A prudent skipper will:

   (a) obtain local knowledge before attempting to run an unfamiliar inlet.
   (b) always run through at top speed.
   (c) find channels well defined and unchanging.
   (d) assume there are no breaking waves when none are visible from sea.

6. Your shortest route to the sea is over a shoal that has a charted depth of 1 foot. Your sailboat has a 5-foot draft. Allowing for a safe water depth of at least 3 feet below the keel and with a height of tide of 6 feet, you can safely pass over the shoal:

   (a) anytime.
   (b) during the time interval from ⅓ the duration before high tide through ⅓ the duration after high tide.
   (c) only at high tide.
   (d) not at all, the water is always too shallow.

7. An ebb *tidal current*:

   (a) causes water to flood the land.
   (b) flows toward land.
   (c) is the current at high tide.
   (d) flows toward the sea.

8. You are 4 miles offshore on a calm day and your engine stops. A quick check of the local current information reveals a flood *current is in effect for the next five hours. You should:*

   (a) drop anchor to prevent drifting farther offshore.
   (b) start paddling.
   (c) let the boat drift toward shore.
   (d) put on a life jacket.

9. A bridge has a 16 foot clearance. Your vessel requires 13 feet to safely pass under the bridge. If the height of tide is 6 feet, you can pass under the bridge:

   (a) anytime.
   (b) from one hour before to one hour after low tide.
   (c) during ⅓ of the duration before through ⅓ of the duration after low tide.
   (d) during ⅓ of the duration before through ⅓ of the duration after high tide.

There are thirty thousand miles of improved waterways in the continental United States, along with thousands of miles of lake shorelines and natural rivers. In many ways, boating on these protected waters may seem more serene than along the coast and for the most part it is. But inland boating has its hazards too. Currents, for example, are encountered not only in tidal estuaries on the coast, but also on streams and even some lakes. River and lake water levels may vary by as much as fifteen feet to cause problems in mooring and docking.

Because rivers drain the surrounding countryside, much debris is carried into the stream. Sometimes logs float just below the surface; sometimes they stand on end and float upright. Avoid this trash because the part you don't see is often larger than that which is visible.

Running rivers can be rugged for other reasons too. Long stretches may offer nothing for the boater's comfort or service. Bridges are not necessarily built to any minimum clearance and you should learn the clearance for any bridge you will encounter on a trip before you get to it; cruising a river requires careful research in advance. Look, too, for the safety harbors established at intervals. They are small, deep-water, protected coves identified on charts.

Dikes and jetties are frequent along rivers; they are designed to let the current shoal the bottom in places that will not interfere with navigation. That keeps shoaling away from the channel. The pilot is advised to keep clear of such jetties.

Which way is which on a river? Facing downstream the right bank is to your right and much information is arranged in a right-bank/left-bank style. The channel is usually on the outer curve of the river at bends, but if it suddenly changes you are warned by a "crossing daymark," a diamond shape in either red or green depending on the side it is on. Daymarks carry on the red-triangle/green-square system and the buoyage system is also the same. The red marks are always on the left bank.

The rules of the road are simple: Keep out of the way of the big tows of barges, usually pushed by tugs. These tows are so big they seem unmaneuverable and they cut off the view so the tug pilot cannot see anything much closer than a half mile. Never dispute a tow for the best channel.

LOCKS

Many rivers, like canals, have locks. The river may include a series of pools dammed, to maintain sufficient depth and traffic must get around the dams by locking through.

The lockmaster is in charge; do what he says and be grateful for any advice he gives. Don't be afraid to tell him you are a greenhorn at locking; he likely will keep watch to help you. He enforces the priority system which has your noncommercial boat at the bottom of the totem pole. He can rule off any boat presenting a danger.

You will need substantial fenders when locking and a half-inch nylon line more than twice as long as the lock's height. That's for tying onto bollards at the top of the lock. If there is a floating bollard the line needs to be only twice your boat's length (fig. 3–1). Do not enter a lock until told to do so and do take the location that the lockmaster designates. You may be in a lock with other boats, so stick to your place along the wall.

Handle the lines to take up slack as you rise or pay out as you descend. Be prepared to coil slack line so you or another crew member will not trip on it. And have a handhold when water is filling or draining the lock. The turbulence is noticeable.

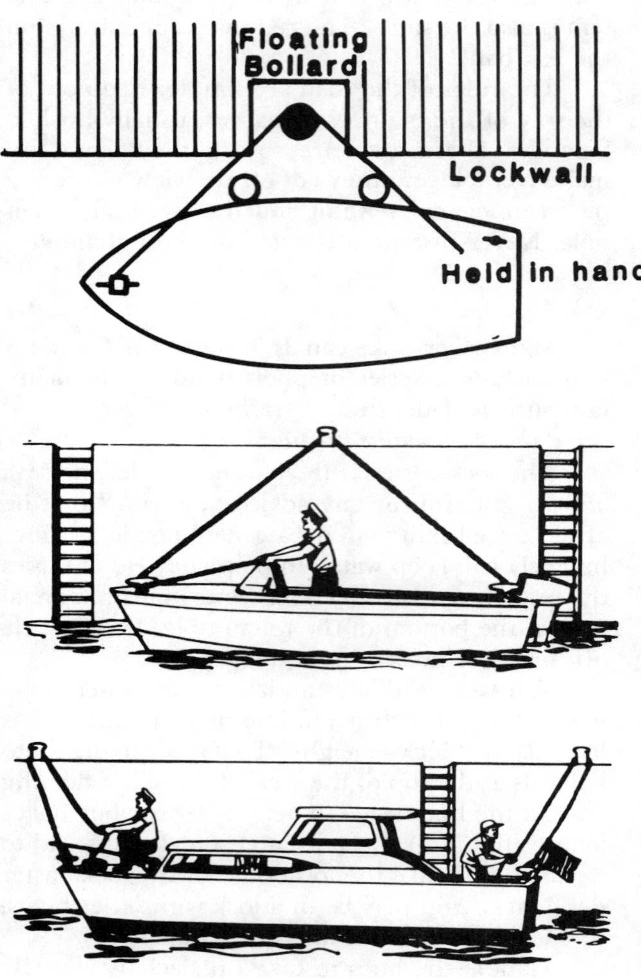

Figure 3-1

Section 3: STUDY QUESTIONS FOR INLAND BOATING

1. Inland boating is different from coastal boating because:
   (a) of conditions during flooding and droughts.
   (b) there are no currents on lakes.
   (c) weather and waves are unimportant on inland waters.
   (d) water levels never change.

2. Red (nun) buoys will be found on rivers on the:
   (a) left side facing downstream.
   (b) same side as they would be for a coastal mariner returning from seaward.
   (c) along the left bank.
   (d) all of the above.

3. Charts or "navigational maps" for inland waters:
   (a) are just like coastal charts.
   (b) usually indicate water level in feet above mean sea level.
   (c) are published by NOAA.
   (d) make the need for other local knowledge unnecessary.

4. When passing under a river bridge, you should:
   (a) know the vertical clearance of the bridge beforehand.
   (b) stay close to shore.
   (c) stay close to side piers to give other boats space to go through.
   (d) speed up to avoid objects falling off of, or thrown from the bridge.

5. Daymarks are:

   (a) either green or red.
   (b) red on the left bank and green on the right bank.
   (c) red on the right bank and green on the left bank.
   (d) not shown on charts.

6. On a bend in a river:

   (a) shoals may form on the outside of the bend.
   (b) you may safely "cut across" the inside of the bend.
   (c) there will be no current on the outside of the bend.
   (d) towboats going downstream usually take the outside bend.

7. Serious hazards to watch for on a river are:

   (a) lee shores downstream from islands.
   (b) logs and other debris.
   (c) shoals on the outside of bends.
   (d) areas of calm water downstream from jetties.

8. When you meet a tow on a river, you should:

   (a) sound three blasts on your horn.
   (b) stay behind him as close as possible.
   (c) stay as far away as possible.
   (d) keep to the right of the channel.

9. On entering a lock, you must:

   (a) tie your boat securely to the cleats on the lock wall.
   (b) obey all instructions of the lockmaster.
   (c) leave the boat until lockage is completed.
   (d) keep your motor running until you can leave the lock.

10. When anchoring in lakes formed by damming rivers, it is a good practice to:

   (a) use an extra heavy anchor.
   (b) use an extra strong anchor rode.
   (c) use a trip line to aid retrieval.
   (d) anchor facing downstream.

The five Great Lakes with their connecting channels provide access to a region notable for its natural and industrial resources. The total water area of the Great Lakes is 95,000 square miles bounded by 8,300 miles of shoreline.

There are three navigable connections to the sea. To the Atlantic Ocean—via the St. Lawrence River from the Gulf of St. Lawrence; or via the New York State Barge Canal System and the Hudson River to New York Harbor. To the Gulf of Mexico—via the Illinois Waterway to the Mississippi River.

CHARTS AND AIDS

Polyconic Charts

Navigational charts published for the Great Lakes are polyconic charts and are different from the more common Mercator charts. On a Mercator chart, parallels of latitude are parallel; meridians of longitude are parallel; and lines of latitude are perpendicular to lines of longitude. Close inspection of polyconic charts will reveal that the lines are not exactly parallel. The central meridian on this chart is a straight line. The other meridians are curved concave toward the central meridian (fig. 3–2). Polyconic charts provide better representation of geographic shapes and features.

The Great Lakes charts record distance in statute miles (5,280 feet). Distance scales are provided in feet, yards, meters, and statute miles. As with a Mercator chart, direction is plotted by using the compass rose closest to your position.

The National Ocean Survey and the Canadian Hydrographic Service planned to produce charts of waters on the U.S.-Canadian boundary

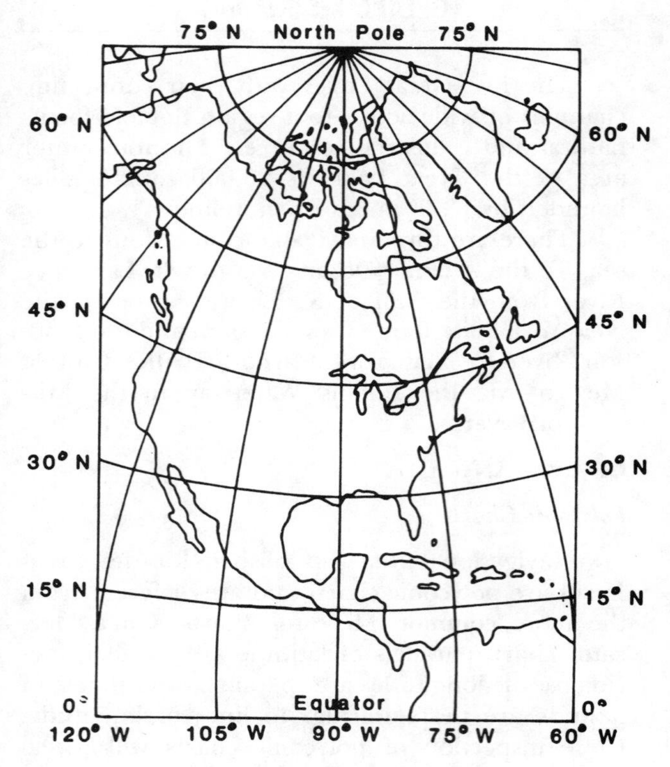

Figure 3-2

with distances and depths in metric units. Several charts of Lakes Erie and Ontario have been produced. These charts are Mercator projections. At this time, the plan is progressing quite slowly and may be expected to continue so in the near future.

Aids to Navigation

The lateral buoyage system on the Great Lakes, in both United States and Canadian waters, is the same as in U.S. coastal waters with respect to shape, coloring, numbering, and light characteristics.

The buoys, however, are colored and numbered as proceeding from the outlet end of each lake. Thus, numbers increase, and red buoys mark the starboard side of the channel when sailing west or north, except on Lake Michigan, where the direction is south.

VISITING CANADA

Regulatory Matters

There are differences in the customs and regulations of the United States and Canada, and although minor, you need to know them. Both the United States and Canada encourage international cruising and regulatory detail is minimal.

However, entering or clearing a country encompasses the areas of public health, agriculture, immigration, and customs. In both Canada and the United States the first contact visiting skippers make is with the Customs Service. Customs officers are versed in matters that could require approval of other agencies and are empowered to make arrangements for all transactions and provide advice.

Before departing the United States, be sure to check requirements for entering Canada:

1. A citizen of any nation except Canada or the United States may require a visa to enter Canada and again to re-enter the United States; this is important because many short-term visitors enter the United States on a single-entry visa. Foreign immigrants to the United States—those with "green cards" certifying immigrant status—are treated as United States citizens relative to going to or coming back from Canada (but they must have their green cards with them).

2. Dogs and cats require rabies certification. Such certification is valid for 3 years. Dogs and cats may have to be kept aboard.
3. Foreign purchases exceeding specified amounts are subject to duty collectible upon re-entry to the United States.
4. Plants, animals, and products thereof are regulated to prevent pests and disease. The United States pays particular attention to live plants in soil. You must declare live plants to United States Customs.
5. Canada is restrictive to the entry of firearms. The United States is sensitive to large amounts of United States currency taken out of the country. Both the United States and Canada limit the amount of tobacco and alcohol that may be imported. The possession of illegal drugs can result in the impounding of your vessel.

There is no need to clear the United States at departure. Once made fast to a dock or anchored in a Canadian harbor, the ship's master is required to contact a Vessel Reporting Station immediately. Passengers and pets must remain aboard until clearance is given by a Customs Officer. Ordinarily, Vessel Report Form E899 will be filed. You will receive a copy, which is your "cruising license" and is good for all Canadian ports that you visit for the duration of your stay as described on that form.

There is no need to clear Canadian Customs when you leave. Upon re-entering the United States, you are required to contact a United States Customs House in person or by telephone. If you have no foreign merchandise aboard subject to duty, you may dismiss your passengers and make the report during the next business day. However, if you have items subject to duty, you should arrange to arrive during business hours or have made prior arrangements with the Customs Officer. The vessel may be directed to an inspection station. Until a Customs Officer gives clearance, passengers should remain aboard.

An annual customs processing fee of $25 is assessable for vessels returning to the United States. This fee may be prepaid, or can be paid upon first arrival. You will receive a customs decal which is good for the rest of the calendar year. If you do not prepay the fee, your first arrival should be during business hours. The fee is associated with the vessel, not the master—if you re-enter in a different boat you will have to pay another fee. The boat keeps her decal regardless of who skippers her.

Regulations are revised periodically. If you plan to cruise in Canadian waters, it is a good idea to determine if any regulations have changed.

Flag Etiquette

Proper observance of the customs and etiquette respecting the ensign, the flag that denotes the nationality of a vessel, becomes more important in an international environment. Fly the U.S. National Ensign (50 stars) from the stern staff. When in Canadian waters, it is a matter of courtesy that you fly the Canadian Ensign, the red and white Maple Leaf flag. There are only two correct places to fly the Canadian Ensign: the starboard spreader, if you have a mast; otherwise, the bow staff. No other flag is appropriate from the same halyard or staff.

Section 3: STUDY QUESTIONS FOR GREAT LAKES BOATING

1. A Great Lakes chart is usually a:
   (a) Mercator projection.
   (b) gnomonic projection.
   (c) transverse Mercator projection.
   (d) polyconic projection.

2. The chart projection used for Great Lakes charts is such that:
   (a) better representation of land shapes and features is achieved.
   (b) the latitude and longitude lines cross at right angles.
   (c) all latitude lines are straight lines.
   (d) all longitude lines are curved lines.

3. When you enter a Canadian harbor:
   (a) you must report to Canadian Customs by the next day.
   (b) you may not permit passengers or pets to disembark until clearance is given by the Customs Officer.
   (c) a visa is required for all on board.
   (d) you do not have to contact Canadian Customs if you have clearance from U.S. Customs.

4. The principal contact between government agencies and international cruising boaters is the:
   (a) Department of Agriculture.
   (b) Federal Maritime Services.
   (c) Customs Service.
   (d) Department of Justice (Immigration).

5. When returning to the U. S. you are required to:

   (a) clear with Canadian Customs before leaving.
   (b) contact U.S. Customs upon re-entry to the U.S.
   (c) do nothing but return to your slip or mooring.
   (d) both a and b.

6. It is customary when in foreign waters to display the ensign of the host country along with the U.S. National Ensign. On a boat without a mast these two ensigns are flown as follows:

   (a) U.S. on the stern staff, Canadian on the bow staff.
   (b) U.S. on the stern staff, Canadian from the radio antenna.
   (c) U.S. on the bow staff, Canadian on the stern staff.
   (d) both on the radio antenna, the U.S. above the Canadian.

7. A sailboat displays the Canadian Ensign from the:

   (a) stern staff.
   (b) starboard spreader.
   (c) port spreader.
   (d) top of the mast.

8. Taking dogs and cats into Canada via boat requires:

   (a) an up-to-date health record.
   (b) a current license tag.
   (c) a valid rabies certificate.
   (d) all the above.

SECTION 4

Basic Navigation and Engine Troubleshooting

THE MARINER'S COMPASS

The basic idea of navigation is to take a vessel that is located at a known site and move it to another known site. The mariner's compass takes care of the critical step of pointing in the correct direction. It has been doing that for sailors for centuries.

As an instrument the compass is a simple device: A card rests on a pivot held by the attraction between the Earth's magnetism and small magnets fixed to the card. Almost all the refinements of the modern compass aim at saving the card and pivot from wear and impairment by the sea's action.

The card is a circular disc of a light, strong nonmagnetic material like aluminum. It is marked in graduated equal divisions of degrees in a full circle. The central pivot is sharp-pointed hard metal. The card is supported by a jeweled cap at its center which rides the pivot point.

This apparatus is mounted in double gimbals so that every effect of sea motion is counteracted by the gimbals, leaving the card to remain horizontal on its jewel bearing. The whole assembly is floated in oil inside a compass bowl to minimize friction at the pivot point and dampen the movement of the card. Marked on the inside of the compass bowl is an index mark called the "lubber's line." In action, as the vessel turns, the lubber's line turns while the card continues to point toward the Earth's magnetic North pole. This is a most difficult concept for the beginner to accept; to him it "looks" as if the card is turning.

When the vessel's turning ceases, the lubber's line points to the number of degrees on the card indicating the new heading.

The magnets (compass card) of the mariner's compass position themselves in response to the earth's magnetism. This is rarely the same direction as True North. The angular difference between True North and the direction of the earth's magnetism is called *variation.* Variation changes with geographic position on earth. In any one location, however, variation is the same for all magnetic compasses on all boats.

The amount and direction of variation are found on a compass rose on the chart; you will find the amount and direction of annual change of variation in the center of the compass rose.

Variation is named east or west. When the earth's magnetic field causes the compass to point westward of True North, variation is west. Conversely, when the earth's field causes the compass to point eastward of True North, variation is east. To determine the magnetic steering course, *subtract east variation* from the magnetic course and *add west deviation.*

The compass is your most important piloting tool, so you should buy the best quality you can manage. It is a good idea to purchase the larger-size compass because it is more stable and tends to be of higher quality than small ones. Your available space may limit size, however. Other things to look for in a compass are quick damping of gyration and accuracy of adjustment magnets. An exterior night light is preferable to an interior one. Keep in mind that excessive heat or light from the sun and extended exposure to cold will eventually damage your compass, so find a way to protect it when it is not in use.

Card markings must be readable. Cardinal points are marked with the letters *N, E, S, W.* The 90-degree spaces between them are subdivided into three 30-degree points marked with a principal line for each 10 degrees. A minor line halves these to 5-degree spaces. The helmsman interpolates the smallest spaces by estimating.

The compass should be mounted on a site that is easily visible to the helmsman and with the lubber line parallel to the keel. It should also be remote from on-board magnetic influences and electric currents. A distance of three feet is usually adequate, but remember—three feet in any direction. A radio set a few inches away on the far side of a thin bulkhead can cause error.

A compass card graduated every 5°. Most helmsmen find this type of graduation easy to use. Reading: 113°.

Figure 4-1

Section 4: STUDY QUESTIONS FOR BASIC NAVIGATION

1. The key factors to consider when selecting a compass are:

   (a) size, color.
   (b) size, space available, quality.
   (c) price, location of the lubber's line.
   (d) size, location of the lubber's line.

2. A compass should be mounted:

   (a) so it is easily visible to the helmsman.
   (b) at least 3 feet from magnetic material.
   (c) with the lubber's line parallel to the boat's keel.
   (d) all of the above.

3. Care of a compass should include avoiding:

   (a) excessive pivot wear and damage due to direct sunlight.
   (b) excessive pivot wear only.
   (c) cold weather use and excessive pivot wear.
   (d) damage due to direct sunlight only.

4. A course line drawn on a chart is labeled as follows:

   (a) course above the course line, distance below the course line.
   (b) distance above the course line, course below the course line.
   (c) course and distance above the course line.
   (d) course and distance below the course line.

5. True Course directions are:

   (a) indicated by letters: N, S, E, W, NE, SE, etc.
   (b) determined by reading your compass.
   (c) measured in degrees from 000 to 359.
   (d) never plotted on a chart.

6. Distance on a nautical chart is determined by:

   (a) using the longitude scale along the bottom of the chart.
   (b) using a course plotter.
   (c) using the latitude scale along the sides of the chart or the distance scale.
   (d) using a ruler.

7. A nautical mile is:

   (a) the same as a statute mile.
   (b) equal to 1 minute of longitude.
   (c) equal to 1 minute of latitude.
   (d) 5,280 feet.

8. Variation:

   (a) changes with geographic position.
   (b) is found on the compass rose of a chart.
   (c) is the angular difference between the True North and Magnetic North directions.
   (d) all of the above.

Use the practice chart and a plotter to solve the next set of problems.

Plot a True Course from buoy R "2" WHISTLE (west of Echo Is.) to bell buoy RG "D" BELL near the LEDGE.

9. The True Course is:

   (a) 165°
   (b) 345°
   (c) 075°
   (d) 355°

10. If the variation is 11° E, the magnetic course will be:

    (a) 154°
    (b) 176°
    (c) 334°
    (d) 356°

11. The distance in nautical miles between the buoys is:

(a) 8.0
(b) 6.1
(c) 5.1
(d) 7.6

Plot a True Course from buoy RG "D" BELL near the LEDGE to the midchannel buoy BELL RW "E" BELL at the mouth of West River.

12. The True Course is:

(a) 087°
(b) 296°
(c) 267°
(d) 356°

13. If the variation is 5° W, the magnetic course will be:

(a) 272°
(b) 089°
(c) 091°
(d) 261°

14. The distance in nautical miles between the buoys is:

(a) 6.8
(b) 4.6
(c) 6.1
(d) 5.0

Plot a True Course from RW "E" BELL to the flashing green light, FLG, at the entrance of FOXTROT POND.

15. The True Course is:

(a) 079°
(b) 241°
(c) 151°
(d) 061°

16. If the variation is 11° E, the magnetic course will be:

(a) 050°
(b) 230°
(c) 090°
(d) 072°

17. The distance of this course in nautical miles is:

(a) 6.5
(b) 5.9
(c) 4.8
(d) 4.1

Plot a True Course from the flashing green light, FLG, at the entrance of FOXTROT POND to RG "D" BELL west of the LEDGE.

18. The True Course is:

(a) 340°
(b) 109°
(c) 160°
(d) 069°

19. If the variation is 5° W, the magnetic course will be:

(a) 165°
(b) 154°
(c) 345°
(d) 254°

20. The distance of this course in nautical miles is:

(a) 2.8
(b) 2.2
(c) 1.2
(d) 3.2

Engine trouble? We will discuss some of the causes of engine failure and suggest some possible cures. The best "cure" is prevention. Take time to make some simple checks before you leave the dock. Do you have enough fuel? Is the oil up to the proper level okay in the engine and transmission or sterndrive unit? Is the battery water all right? Do the belts have correct tension? Is there excessive water in the bilge? Do all the hoses appear to be okay? Once under way, glance at your gauges or indicator lights occasionally to catch signs of trouble.

If the engine stops while under way, the first thing to remember is *don't panic.* The trouble is usually simple. Look around and assess your situation, remembering that the safety of your passengers and your boat is your prime concern.

If you are in open water and can drift without getting into danger (such as drifting out to sea), post a lookout and then start looking for what caused the engine to stop. If it is windy and the water is rough, put out an anchor from the bow to hold the boat into the wind to stabilize it and increase your comfort. On rivers with a current, you might want to anchor at once to keep the boat from drifting aground or into a bridge abutment or other hazard. If there is commercial traffic nearby, try to drift or otherwise get out of the channel before anchoring. Tows and large vessels cannot stop quickly and have limited maneuvering ability.

When your boat is safe, consider the engine problem. This section covers the engine problems you are most likely to encounter and suggests solutions that may help you get home safely. The basic causes of engine failure relate to problems in one or more of the following fundamental systems: (1) fuel system; (2) cooling system; (3) ignition system.

GASOLINE INBOARD ENGINES

Fuel System Problems

Fuel system problems may be caused by water or dirt particles in the fuel or by the engine not receiving any fuel at all. The engine with fuel system problems usually coughs or sputters before finally stopping. A typical fuel system is shown in figure 4–2.

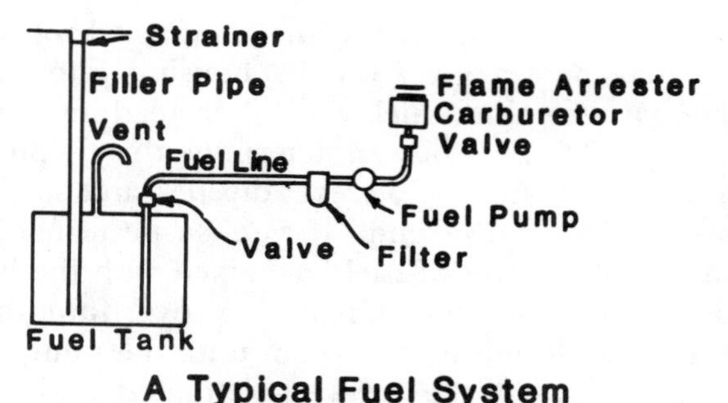

A Typical Fuel System

Figure 4-2

If the fuel system is suspect, the first thing to do is to be sure there is fuel in the tank(s) and that any tank valves have not inadvertently been turned off. The valve that should be located near the engine should also be checked. Most fuel tanks are constructed so that fuel is not picked up directly from the bottom of the tank, thus preventing condensed moisture from being pulled into the fuel system.

The next thing to do is find out if fuel is reaching and passing through the carburetor to the intake manifold. Since most engines have the carburetor mounted on or near the top of the engine, the easiest way to be sure that fuel is getting through is to operate the throttle a few times at the helm and then quickly remove the flame arrestor from the top of the carburetor and look directly down into it. If the inside surfaces appear wet, fuel is probably getting to the engine. If the inside surfaces are dry, operate the throttle again with the flame arrestor off, watching the carburetor. If everything still looks dry, fuel is probably not getting through. This can be caused by clogged filters or strainers or by a broken fuel pump.

Broken Fuel Pump. If the fuel pump is broken, fuel may be leaking from its housing into the bilge. Or sometimes fuel will leak instead into the engine crankcase. You can determine this by pulling out the crankcase oil level dipstick and smelling the oil on the end. If you suspect that a substantial amount of fuel has mixed with the lubricating oil (the dipstick may show over full), the engine should not be run again until the pump is fixed, the oil in the crankcase drained and replaced, and the oil filter changed. Some fuel pumps have a diaphragm that can be replaced easily if it fails, but it is more common today to replace the entire pump.

Clogged Filters. If there is no indication that the fuel pump has failed, then clogged filters or strainers are probably preventing fuel from getting to the engine. Some engines have sediment bowls, either as an integral part of the fuel pump or mounted separately in the fuel lines. They may contain a metal mesh or ceramic filter that has become clogged. Removing the bowl will allow the filter to be removed for cleaning. Sometimes it is not possible to clean the ceramic type without a strong solvent, so just leaving it out may solve the problem long enough to get you home. Be sure that the bowl seals well on its gasket when it is reinstalled (fig. 4–3). Some carburetors have a filter built right in where the fuel line enters. This is usually the pleated paper type of filter, which cannot be easily cleaned; in a pinch, it too can be left out, or its filtering ability can be aborted by punching a hole through the filter media to let the fuel pass.

Closed Choke. When you first took the flame arrestor off the top of the carburetor, the choke butterfly plate should have been at least part way open if the engine has been run enough to get it warm. If it is all the way closed, you will not be able to see down into the carburetor. The engine is probably flooding out because the choke is closed to cause enrichment of the air-fuel mixture—desirable for easy starting in cold weather, but very undesirable for a warm engine.

Most automatic chokes prevent the butterfly from moving if the throttle is closed, so advance the throttle a bit before attempting to work the butterfly by hand. If it is sticky or gummy, just opening it by hand may be the solution to getting you home where the problem can be solved correctly. If it will not stay open because of some mechanical problem try to wire or tie it open on the outside of the carburetor.

NOTE: Never put anything down into a carburetor that is small enough to pass clear through. It could cause severe engine damage.

After wiring or tying the butterfly open, you should operate the throttle slowly once or twice to be sure that this will not cause damage to other linkages.

Water in Fuel. If fuel is getting through to the engine, yet the problem still appears to be in the fuel system, there may be water mixed with the fuel. If the seas have been rough or choppy, any water that is in the tank may have been stirred up and mixed with the fuel and then carried into the engine where it may not burn because of the mixture's lowered volatility. If this is suspected, then the fuel filters or sediment bowls (fig. 4–3) should be checked. If water is present, gasoline will be floating on top of the water or the water will appear as bubbles in the bottom of the bowl. If water is found, the bowl or cup should be emptied (not overboard), the bowl replaced, and the engine started. The engine should run for a long time before the filter has to be cleaned again, but it should be checked frequently.

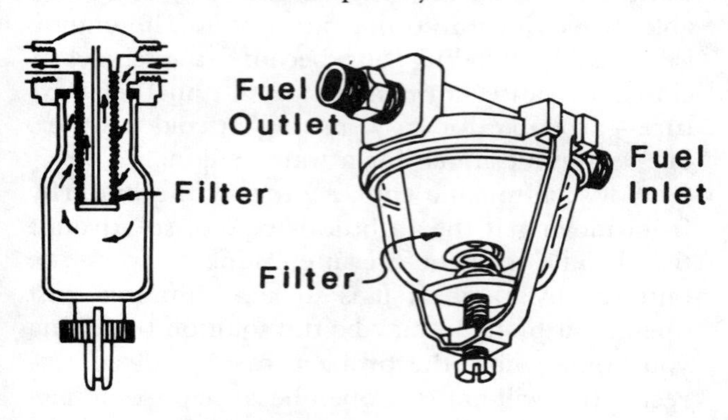

Sediment Bowl Type Filter

Figure 4-3

Back at your home port or the nearest marina, depending on the urgency of the problem, the contaminated fuel should be pumped out and replaced with fresh. Sometimes it is not possible to get all of the water out of the tank so it is wise to put some automotive gas-line deicer or plain alcohol (not more than 10 percent by volume) in with the new fuel to absorb and burn the remaining water.

NOTE: ALWAYS USE EXTREME CAU-

TION WHEN WORKING ON ANY PART OF THE FUEL SYSTEM: A SMALL AMOUNT OF FUEL SPILLED ON A HOT ENGINE OR IGNITED BY A SPARK CAN CREATE A DEADLY HOLOCAUST.

Cooling System Problems

When the engine stopped, did you look at your temperature gauge to see if the engine was running hot? If it was and the engine stopped because of this, there could be several reasons.

Broken Belt. One of the most common causes is a broken or stretched belt. When a belt has stretched to the point that it will no longer drive its load, increasing tension may damage its internal cords and cause it to break in a short time. You may, however, be able to add some slight tension so that it will drive the pump at idle speed; then by going slowly you may be able to limp home. Any acceleration of the engine may cause the belt to snap. If the engine has other belt-driven accessories, you may be able to pirate a belt, such as the one for the alternator. An engine will run for a long time on a fully charged battery if other things are not draining its power. Sometimes a little ingenuity will take you a long way.

Most marine engines today are based on automotive or industrial designs that were highly developed before they were used in marine service. Consequently, the cooling system of a marine engine is likely to be much like the original. The standard water circulating pump is used and the thermostat is located in the same place. So the most common means of getting cooling water to the engine circulating pump and to the exhaust manifolds is to add a separate pump as an accessory and drive it by an additional belt from the crankshaft pulley (fig. 4–4). Many times the engine circulating pump (which is fixed in one place) and the alternator are driven by a single belt, with the alternator mounted with a pivot point so that it can be used to tension the belt. With this arrangement it is possible to have two concurrent problems—a hot engine and a dead battery—if a broken belt goes undetected.

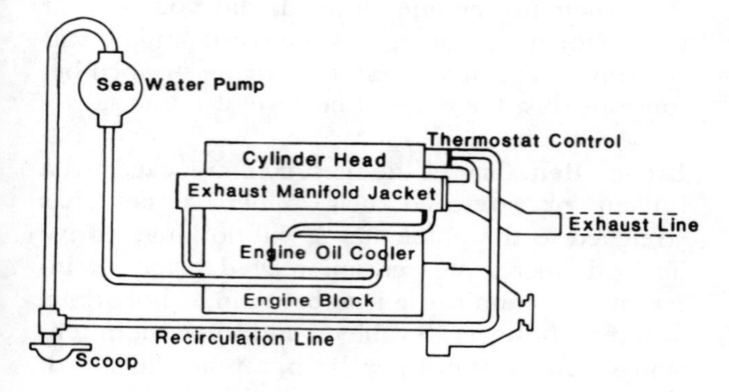

Direct Cooling System

Figure 4-4

Pump or Thermostat. An engine that stopped because it was too hot will usually restart after it has cooled; in that case, check the exhaust outlets to see that the cooling water is exiting there as it should. For sterndrive units with underwater exhaust, you will have to tip the unit up until the exhaust outlet is above the water to make this check. If cooling water is coming out, it can be assumed that the sea water pump is working. This could mean that the engine circulating pump has failed or that the thermostat has failed to open to allow the necessary flow of cooling water. (Note that a thermostat can also fail in the fully open position which will cause an engine to run colder than it should.)

The easiest way to correct a problem thermostat is to remove it temporarily. The worst part about this job is that more often than not the gasket that seals the thermostat housing to the block will be damaged or destroyed. It is possible to make a temporary gasket from any thin cardboard or flexible plastic. If the engine circulating pump has failed (a rare occurrence), it will probably be leaking water around its drive shaft. You can usually do nothing about this but try to get home by running at slow speed while keeping a wary eye on the temperature gauge.

Blocked Water Intake. If no cooling water was coming from the exhaust outlets, then either the sea water pump has failed or the water intake is blocked. Sterndrive units will probably have water pickup slots located in the leading edge of the lower unit housing, and these can be checked for blockage by tilting the unit up out of the water. Often this is the only action required—whatever was causing the blockage may just fall off. On a straight inboard engine, you may have to duck under the boat to see if the intake scoop is blocked. Before you do that though, check its location from inside the boat. Again, since there is suction on the inlet with the engine running, just stopping the engine might allow the debris to fall off. Plastic bags are common items that block engine cooling water intakes.

Failed Impeller. If there are no blockages, yet no cooling water is being exhausted, the impeller in the sea water pump has failed. It is a multi-fingered rubber piece mounted eccentrically inside a circular housing. As it rotates in the housing, the fingers are alternately flexed and extended with each revolution of the shaft, and eventually they wear out and break off. When many of these fingers are missing, the pump will no longer pump enough water to keep the engine cooled, and the impeller must be replaced. If you do not have a spare, you may have to get a tow.

Engine oil cools as well as lubricates, so always be sure that the crankcase is filled to the proper level. If oil pressure suddenly drops—STOP THE ENGINE AT ONCE. Pull out the dipstick, wipe it off, and reinsert it; then pull it out again and read it. If you need oil, add the correct amount and check for leaks after you restart the engine.

Ignition System Problems

If the engine stopped abruptly, there may be an ignition system problem.

Poor Contact. The first place to look for ignition trouble is the large wire that leads from the center of the distributor cap to the ignition coil (fig. 4–5). (On some of the newer transistorized ignition systems, the coil is built inside the distributor cap, so this check is not possible.) If the wire is loose in its socket at either end, the engine will not run. An end that seems loose should be pulled out and examined because looseness at these terminals often causes the end of the wire to burn away as a result of arcing. This can be corrected in a wire with a metal center conductor by stripping the insulation off about 1 inch of good center conductor, then folding the center conductor up along the insulation still on the wire. In this way it will make a solid contact when it is plugged back into its socket.

Many high-voltage wires now in use do not use metal as the center conductor but have nylon fibers impregnated with carbon. This wire is used because of its superior radio non-interference characteristics. Contact between the center con-

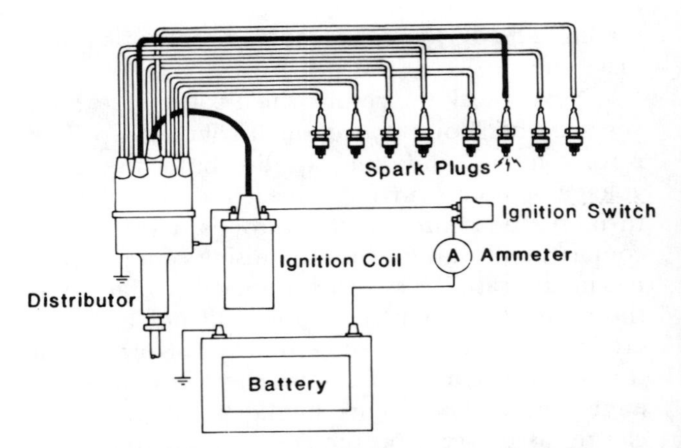

Figure 4-5

ducting fibers and the socket is usually made by a metal wire that is shaped something like a long staple. One leg of the staple is inserted into the center conductor and the other leg makes contact with the terminal on the outside of the wire. These wires can also sometimes be repaired temporarily by pulling out the staple, cutting off the wire, and reinserting the staple.

Cracked Cap. Be certain that all spark plug wires are pushed tightly down on the plugs and also down into their sockets in the distributor cap. If they are all making good contact, check the distributor cap for cracks. A virtually invisible crack in the cap material will allow moisture to collect and cause the high-voltage ignition current to be shunted off to ground, or to another terminal where it can cause the wrong spark plug to fire.

Once current has passed through a crack, it will normally continue because the arcing leaves carbon particles that conduct electrical current readily. The only solution to this problem is to replace the cap.

Next, check the rotor, which is the first thing you see when you remove the distributor cap. The rotor rotating inside the cap distributes the high-voltage ignition current to each spark plug in turn. In the center of the rotor is a spring-like contact point that touches the inside center terminal in the cap. This spring should be intact, and the rotating outer metal tip should not be badly eroded or the rotor must be replaced. Now look at the breaker points while someone else cranks the engine over. The points should be opening and closing as the cam on the center shaft rotates. If they are not opening at all, they must be adjusted. The engine should be turned over and stopped repeatedly until one of the high spots on the center shaft cam is resting almost exactly on the plastic rubbing block. Loosen the point locking screw and set a gap the thickness of a matchbook cover (about .016 inch) between the contacts. Later, at a yard or marina, they should be properly set. If the points show evidence of pitting, they should be replaced.

Summary

Most gasoline engine problems are related to the fuel, cooling, or ignition systems. Trouble can also result from abusing an engine by running it too fast for long periods or by abusing the reverse gear transmission or sterndrive unit. The first indication of trouble is often a change in the sound of the engine while it is running. Any new sound should be investigated immediately.

GASOLINE OUTBOARD ENGINES

The main difference between inboard and outboard engines is that the inboards have a four-stroke cycle system with a crankcase oil reservoir for lubrication, and most outboards have a two-stroke cycle system with no crankcase oil lubrication. The outboards are normally lubricated by oil mixed with the gasoline. Lubricating systems are sometimes available with remote reservoirs and an injection system that will automatically mix the correct amount of oil with the gasoline at all times. The inboard and outboard have basically the same primary problem areas—the fuel, cooling, and ignition systems.

Fuel System Problems

Fuel system problems can include lack of fuel, improper gasoline-oil mixture, or just dirty fuel. A portable metal fuel tank that has been around salt water for a while may have rusted, with sediment clogging fuel lines and filters.

If the engine was running nicely, then died, sputtered, and stopped, check your fuel tank. Is the fuel line securely connected to the engine and to the tank? Sometimes it looks as if it is when it is not. Are there any cracks in the fuel hose? Squeeze the primer bulb in the hose rapidly several times to be sure that there is pressure and that fuel has been delivered to the carburetor(s)

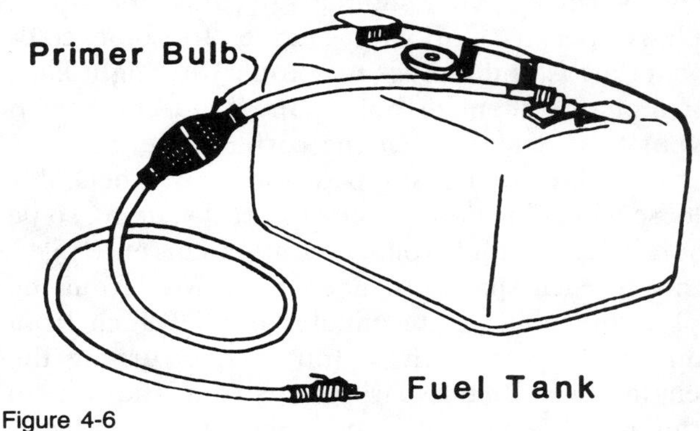

Figure 4-6

(fig. 4–6). Make sure that the tank vent is open so that air can enter to replace the fuel as it is used. If you cannot find a vent, remove the filler cap. If air rushes in, the vent hole is clogged and must be opened before the engine will operate properly.

Water in the gasoline will cause a problem if the quantity is great enough. If this is suspected, the quickest solution may be to switch to a different tank. If the engine runs well on the new tank, the first one should be drained and refilled with fresh, clean fuel. Do not discard the contaminated fuel overboard! This is illegal and dangerous; the discarded fuel will float and could cause a serious fire for you or someone else.

Ignition System Problems

Fouled spark plugs are the most frequent cause of outboard engine ignition problems. This usually occurs when the engine is run at idle for long periods. The reason is that an idling engine is running much cooler and requires a richer fuel mixture than when it is running fast. This is usually not a problem if the engine has surface-gap spark plugs, a capacitive ignition system, fixed jet carburetor(s), and a high fuel-to-oil ratio.

Normally, you should use only the spark plugs specified for your engine. In some cold-water areas, these plugs may foul. You might have to upgrade them to hotter ones, but check with your boat dealer to get the correct type.

If the engine stopped suddenly, check for loose wires throughout the electrical system. To be sure that the high-voltage ignition current is getting to each spark plug, remove a wire from the plug and hold the terminal about 1/8 inch from any metal part of the engine, while turning the engine over. If no spark jumps from the wire to the metal, you may have a magneto problem, which will have to be repaired by a mechanic. Failure of the capacitive-discharge or transistor type ignitions will also usually require a mechanic.

Cooling System Problems

Check the location of the cooling water overflow vent on your outboard engine. If no water comes out of this hole when you start the engine, stop immediately. The water intake is similar to that of the sterndrive unit; check to be sure that it is clear (fig. 4–7). If it is, the cooling water pump has failed and will have to be replaced by a mechanic.

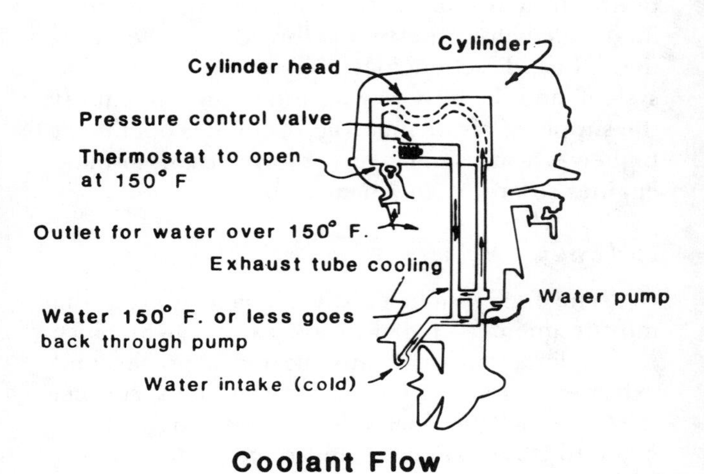

Coolant Flow

Figure 4-7

Summary

Outboard marine engines generally have fewer moving parts, are lighter in weight, and produce more horsepower per pound of weight than the four-stroke cycle gasoline or diesel engines. They are less adaptable for jury-rigging (a solution to get you home in a pinch). Therefore, if you do have problems, check systematically for possible causes. Do not make hasty adjustments or just start taking things apart. Check the simple things first and you will usually find the trouble.

DIESEL INBOARD ENGINES

Diesel engines are produced in both four-stroke cycle and two-stroke cycle configurations, and both are in wide use. In a gasoline engine the fuel-air mixture burns when it is ignited by the high-voltage ignition system. In a diesel engine, on the other hand, the fuel-air mixture is ignited by the heat produced from high compression of intake air before the fuel is forced into the cylinder. Thus, diesel engines do not have an ignition system, and the only way to stop them is to cut off the supply of air or fuel. Diesel engines operate at higher pressures and temperatures than gasoline engines so are usually heavier built.

Fuel System Problems

The fuel system of the diesel engine is the most frequent source of problems (fig. 4–8). Since each cylinder in turn must be fed a precise and extremely minute amount of fuel at an exact time, the parts in the fuel injection system must be made to close tolerances and remain that way for efficient operation. This requires that the fuel be extremely clean when it gets to the main metering pump or injector. In most cases a diesel will have several filters in its fuel supply line since it is much easier to filter out the dirt than it is to clean out the system.

Lack of fuel can result if either the supply or injection pump is broken or if the unit injectors are plugged. Air trapped inside the fuel system

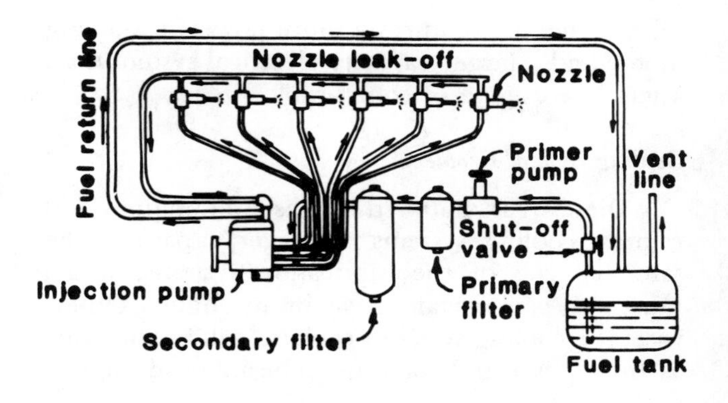

Typical Diesel System

Figure 4-8

can also cause this problem, as can blocked fuel filters requiring bleeding the fuel lines. Algae can grow in diesel fuel that stands for a long time without treatment, and can also clog filters, pumps, and injectors. Special additives should be added to the fuel at each refueling to avoid this problem. If the filters clog up, the engine usually loses power, and the filters should be cleaned or changed at once.

During cold weather, the main reason that a diesel refuses to start (or stops while running) is that low temperatures have caused the fuel to thicken and paraffin has begun to form in it. This readily clogs filters and can damage the injector pump. A diesel usually is equipped with a means to help it start easier. Some diesels have glow plugs in each cylinder that help ignite the fuel in a cold engine, and sometimes the engine has a means of preheating the incoming air. Fuel line heaters are used to melt any paraffin before it can reach the injector pump and cause damage.

Because of the higher compression in a diesel, it generally requires a more powerful starting motor and a larger capacity electrical system than a gasoline engine of comparable size.

Cooling System Problems

Diesels run hotter than gasoline engines and require cooling systems of larger capacity. The same is true of the lubrication systems, which must also cool certain areas in an engine. Otherwise, the cooling system problems will be the same as those discussed for a gasoline inboard engine.

Ignition System Problems

One fundamental advantage of diesel engines is that they have no ignition system and therefore have none of the problems gasoline engines have relating to the maintenance or malfunction of electrical ignition systems.

Summary

Since a diesel uses compression to heat the air in the cylinders to a temperature that will ignite the fuel when it is injected, anything that causes this pressure to be less than it should be will keep the engine from running. Sources of this trouble are worn piston rings, leaking valves or head gaskets, and leaks around injectors or glow plugs. If the fuel is correct and clean and the fuel system is in good working order, most diesel engines will run for thousands of hours without problems.

SPARE PARTS AND TOOLS

Whether you need to carry spare parts on your boat depends on the way you go boating. If you hardly ever get out of sight of your dock or ramp, you may not need to carry any spares. On longer trips, you may want to carry everything that you could possibly ever need. The purpose is to make emergency repairs and get back home, so it is not necessary that parts be new. Many, such as spark plugs, ignition points, distributor rotor, or distributor cap, may be old ones that were removed from your engine the last time it was tuned up.

If you think you need spare parts, it is certain that you need a small kit of tools aboard so you can make emergency repairs. A survey of your engine and boat will indicate what size wrenches and screwdrivers to include. Add adjustable locking pliers, an adjustable wrench, and some wire cutting pliers. A copy of the instruction book or service manual for your engine can be invaluable and should be checked when problems arise.

A little time spent at the pier going over your engine with this section of the course and your engine manual in hand will familiarize you with the location of most of the items that can cause trouble.

When All Else Fails

If you find that you can not get your engine restarted, ask for help. Do not be embarrassed about this—most boatmen have had to do it at one time or another, and most are willing to give someone else a hand.

The recommended signal for help from a small boat is to stand as high as possible and face the other boat with your arms extended out from your sides. Raise your arms over your head and lower them to horizontal repeatedly. You may also cup your hands around your mouth, as though you are yelling, so other boaters understand that you are trying to tell them something.

In the "Required Equipment" Section, it was noted that you must carry distress signals for use in a serious situation. Being out of fuel is not normally considered a serious emergency, so if you ask the Coast Guard for help, you may be charged for that service. Or more likely, if your situation is not life-threatening, your request will be referred to a commercial company which will most certainly charge for services rendered. Learn to be self-reliant and practice prevention. You may save more than just money.

Section 4: STUDY QUESTIONS FOR ENGINE TROUBLESHOOTING

1. Now that you have had your I/O boat for about 6 months, you have developed considerable confidence in it and in yourself. On a beautiful Saturday you and your family are powering across a large lake. Suddenly the motor coughs, loses power, sputters, and stops. You would first:

   (a) check the ignition system.
   (b) check your fuel supply.
   (c) check cooling system.
   (d) look around to check the wind, current, nearby boats, and hazards.

2. When your engine stops you note there is a wind at about 12 mph and a current which will cause you to drift toward a small rocky island, you next decide to:

   (a) begin your investigation of the problem.
   (b) call the Coast Guard.
   (c) anchor.
   (d) look for another boat which you can ask for help.

3. When you raise the engine box cover to check your stalled engine, you notice the engine seems much hotter than usual. You have no temperature gauge, so you decide to:

   (a) check the oil level first.
   (b) check the water pump belt.
   (c) check the distributor cap.
   (d) none of the above.

4. Checking for the cause of overheating, you find that the oil level, alternator belt, and distributor cap are all satisfactory. Before going further, you stop to weigh other possible causes:

   (a) dirt in the fuel filter.
   (b) blockage of the cooling system.
   (c) a loose ignition wire.
   (d) all of the above.

5. Despite the overheating problem, you wonder what caused the engine to cough and sputter to a stop. You decide to check the fuel filter and find that it has dirt in the bottom and about a quarter inch of water. You would:

   (a) empty the bowl overboard and replace it.
   (b) remove the filter screen and replace the bowl, being careful not to spill anything out of the bowl.
   (c) use a rag to soak up the fuel and water, then hang the rag outside where it will dry, away from people, hot exhausts, etc.
   (d) empty it in the bottom of the boat.

6. After removing water and dirt from the filter bowl, you replace the filter bowl and try the engine. It starts, but you realize that you haven't corrected the overheating. You would:

   (a) leave the engine cover up and start home.
   (b) remove the thermostat and start home.
   (c) run the engine in neutral at idle speed, and check the water outlets.
   (d) check the oil level again.

7. You are sailing with a friend in his 18-foot sailboat. The wind drops, so he furls the mainsail, starts the 6-hp outboard motor, and heads for home. After a few minutes, the motor sputters and dies. He should:

   (a) check the fuel supply.
   (b) get a tow from a passing boat.
   (c) sail home with the jib.
   (d) anchor.

8. When your outboard motor sputters and stops, you check the fuel tank and find that the vent screw on the tank cap was closed. This cut off the fuel to the motor because:

   (a) it prevented the gas fumes from escaping.
   (b) it prevented air from entering the tank.
   (c) it cut off the air supply to the carburetor.
   (d) all of the above.

9. You are on a summer cruise in your boat which has a single diesel engine. The weather is stormy and the seas are running high, tossing the boat viciously. Suddenly the engine dies. You decide to anchor and:

   (a) ride out the storm, then clean or change filters and bleed the fuel line.
   (b) check the alternator and the battery water.
   (c) thoroughly check the ignition system.
   (d) clean the paraffin from the injector pump.

SECTION 5

Piloting and Sailing

SPEED, TIME, AND DISTANCE CALCULATIONS

So far you have learned to lay a course line from where you are to where you want to be. You can read the chart to make sure you will not go aground en route. You can measure a true angle course on the chart grid with a plotter, and then convert the true course to a compass course. Dividers and the nearby latitude scale will tell you how many miles you must go. But how long will it take you? When can you expect to be there? How fast do you have to go to make a rendezvous at the appointed hour?

These questions can be answered with the help of a simple formula:

$$60 \times D = S \times T$$

This equation will answer all your questions about distance, speed, and time because D = distance in nautical miles (nm), S = speed in knots (kn), and T = time in minutes. You will need to use twenty-four-hour time; it makes the subtraction easier. For example, let's say you want to know how long a trip will take if a boat leaves at 0912 and arrives at 1547.

Arrive	1547
Depart	−0912
	0635 (6 hours and 35 minutes)

With 60 as a constant, and two of the variables known, you can always find the missing figure. The statement can be rearranged to find any one of them thus:

$$D = \frac{S \times T}{60}$$

$$S = \frac{60 \times D}{T}$$

$$T = \frac{60 \times D}{S}$$

Use this equation to check your answer: $60 \times D = S \times T$

Note that miles and knots are carried to one decimal place (the nearest tenth of a unit) but time is rounded to the nearest whole minute.

PLOTTING EXERCISE

Work through the following problem, using the Sample Plotting Sheet (fig. 5–1). Measure the courses and bearings with the plotter, and measure the distances with dividers.

Beginning at the 0815 Fix at buoy "A," head for buoy "B."

1. What is the True Course? Ans. 100°.
2. What is the magnetic course, if variation is 10° W?

True Course		100°
Variation	(+)	10° W
Magnetic Course		110°

3. What is the distance of the run? 7.4 nm.
4. What speed is required to arrive at 0900?

$$S = \frac{60 \times 7.4}{(0900-0815)} = \frac{60 \times 7.4}{45} = 9.9 \text{ kn}$$

5. At 0838 the boat is stopped and turned toward the spire. A magnetic bearing of 343° is read with the compass. Variation is 10° W. What is the True Bearing?

Magnetic Bearing		343°
Variation	(−)	10° W
True Bearing		333°

What is the 0838 DR position? First find the distance run from 0815 to 0838:

$$D = \frac{9.9 \times (0838-0815)}{60} = \frac{9.9 \times (23)}{60} = 3.8 \text{ nm}$$

Measure along the 100-degree course line 3.8 nautical miles and plot the 0838 DR.

6. At 0900 at buoy "B," change course to 150° True and speed to 8.6 knots. At 0916 change course again to 230° True. Plot these two courses.

a. Plot the True Course of 150° from "B."
b. Determine the 0916 DR by calculating the distance run before making the turn to a True Course of 230°.

$$D = \frac{8.6 \times (0916-0900)}{60} = \frac{8.6 \times (16)}{60} = 2.3 \text{ nm}$$

With dividers, measure 2.3 nautical miles and plot the 0916 DR ending the 150-degree course line. Then plot the 230-degree course line from this point.

7. At 0933 a buoy is abeam (perpendicular to the

course line) to starboard. Draw the LOP and plot the 0933 DR. Draw the LOP from the buoy perpendicular to the course line. Since a magnetic bearing was not determined and the buoy is close aboard, only time is shown above the LOP.

To plot the 0933 DR, determine the distance run from the 0916 DR.

$$D = \frac{8.6 \times (0933 - 0916)}{60} = \frac{8.6 \times (17)}{60} = 2.4 \text{ nm}$$

Measure 2.4 nautical miles along the 230-degree course line and plot the 0933 DR.

8. At 0953, with the boat stopped and headed toward the lighthouse, the compass reads 100°; then with the boat headed toward the tower, the compass reads 185°. Variation is 10° W.

What are the True Bearings of these observations?
Plot the LOPs.

		Lighthouse	Tower
Magnetic Bearing		100°	185°
Variation	(−)	10° W	10° W
		090	175

What is the 0953 DR?

$$D = \frac{8.6 \times (0953 - 0933)}{60} = \frac{8.6 \times (20)}{60} = 2.9 \text{ nm}$$

Measure 2.9 nautical miles along the 230-degree course line from the 0933 DR and plot the 0953 DR.

Plot and label the 0953 Fix.

The 0953 Fix is the point where the two LOPs cross and is marked by a small circle and the time, 0953.

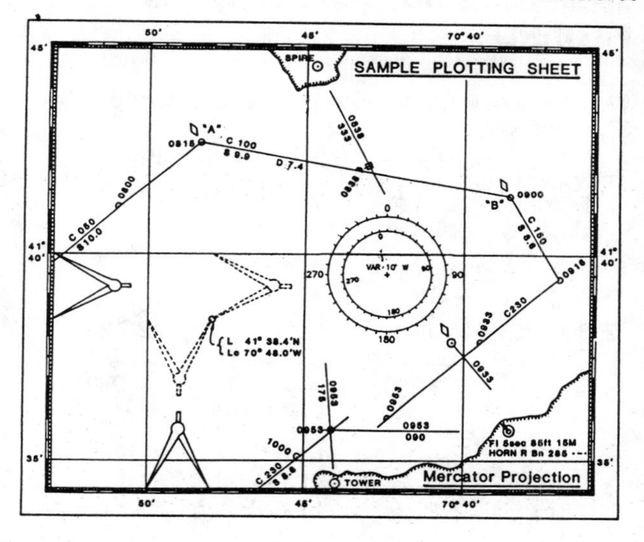

Figure 5-1

Note that the Fix is not on the course line. Wind, current, and other factors usually prevent steering the DR course exactly, hence the importance of periodically checking your position. A new course line is started from the Fix since that is considered a "known" position.

The practice exercises that follow review only the basic principles discussed in this section. If you expect to cruise extensively, additional study of Chapman's, chs. 17, 19, and 20, is recommended.

Section 5: STUDY QUESTIONS FOR PILOTING

Work the following practice problems using the 60D = ST equations:

1.	(a)	(b)	(c)
Speed	_____ kn	_____ kn	_____ kn
Distance	8.0 nm	9.0 nm	22.5 nm
Time	48 min	54 min	_____ min (1 hr 42 min)

2.	(a)	(b)	(c)
Speed	6.0 kn	11.4 kn	12.0 kn
Distance	_____ nm	_____ nm	_____ nm
Time	46 min	_____ min (1 hr 24 min)	55 min

3.	(a)	(b)	(c)
Speed	6.0 kn	12.0 kn	18.4 kn
Distance	5.8 nm	14.8 nm	16.7 nm
Time	_____ min	_____ min	_____ min
	___ hr ___ min	___ hr ___ min	___ hr ___ min

4. Convert the following to nautical time:

   (a) 8:35 a.m. _______ (c) 6:25 a.m. _______
   (b) 11:51 p.m. _______ (d) 3:34 p.m. _______

5. Convert the following to conventional time:

   (a) 0007 _______ (c) 0638 _______
   (b) 2221 _______ (d) 1838 _______

6. What nautical time will it be 47 minutes later than each of the following times listed?

   (a) 11:51 a.m. _______ (d) 2357 _______
   (b) 11:51 p.m. _______ (e) 0007 _______
   (c) 1021 _______

7. What is the elapsed nautical time in the following examples?

	Departure	*Arrival*	*Elapsed Time*
(a)	0835	1052	____________
(b)	1327	1601	____________
(c)	0929	1015	____________
(d)	1843	1901	____________

8. Determine the missing True or Magnetic Course in each of the following examples:

	(a)	(b)	(c)	(d)
T	250	085	______	______
V	10 W	15 E	10 E	5 W
M	______	______	025	325

9. Determine the magnetic variation in each of the following examples. Be sure to indicate the direction:

	(a)	(b)	(c)	(d)
T	135	246	005	043
V	______	______	______	______
M	140	235	355	048

10. What are the longitude and latitude of the following points on the practice chart (at the back of this text and used in "Charts And Aids To Navigation)?

(a) RG "D" BELL near the LEDGE L ____________
Lo ____________

(b) ZULU REEF light L ____________
Lo ____________

(c) Lighthouse on BRAVO POINT L ____________
Lo ____________

On the practice chart (at the back of this text and used with "Charts And Aids To Navigation), plot and label the following courses. Speed is 6.0 knots and Variation is 11° E.

11. From RW "E" BELL at the mouth of West River to R "2" WHISTLE south of ZULU REEF light:

    (a) True Course? ______________________
    (b) Magnetic Course? ______________________
    (c) Distance? ______________________
    (d) Running Time? ______________________
    (e) ETA departing at 0900? ______________________

12. At 0935 you decide to change course for RW "F" BELL at the mouth of East River:

    (a) True Course? ______________________
    (b) Magnetic Course? ______________________
    (c) Distance? ______________________
    (d) Running Time? ______________________
    (e) ETA? ______________________
    (f) Location of 0935 DR? L ____________
    Lo ____________

The most proficient sailors have acquired both knowledge and skill. Some knowledge of sailing theory will also help skippers of powerboats. For example, learning that a sailboat has to tack when going up wind will explain why a sailboat is restricted in maneuverability and, as a consequence, has been given the right-of-way.

HOW A BOAT SAILS

Wind and Sails

The energy that propels a sailboat through the water is the wind, and the device that converts this energy movement is the sails.

One thing common to all sail geometry is the draft of the sail. To understand how the draft produces the drive to move the boat, consider the airfoil, or "airplane wing" section (fig. 5–2.)

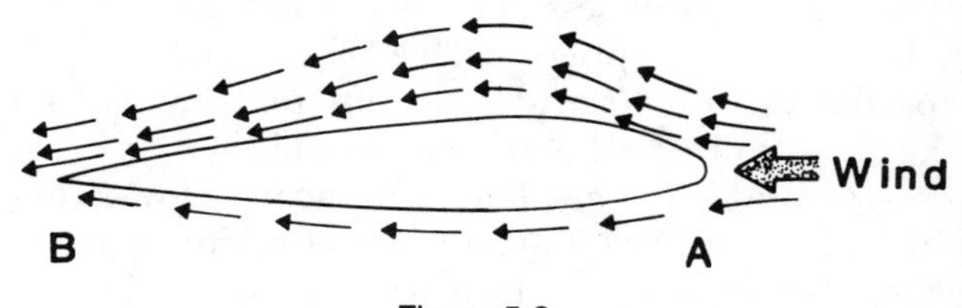

Figure 5-2

Imagine two particles of air arriving at point "A" at the same instant. Then further imagine that they separate, with one particle going over the top of the airfoil while the other goes under the bottom of it. In theory, they will meet again at "B," arriving there at the same time. In order to do so the particle passing along the upper surface of the airfoil must travel a greater distance and

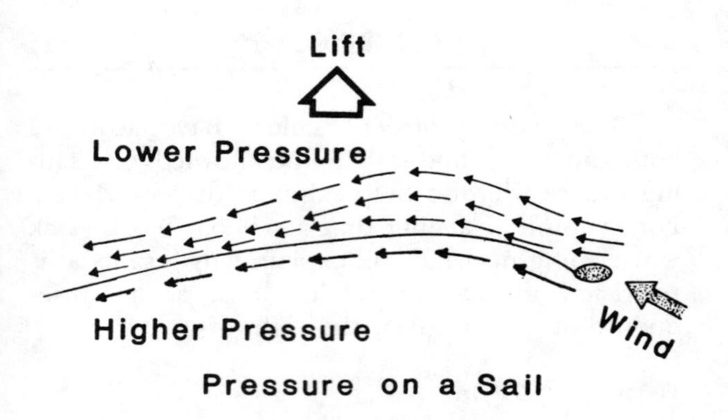

Figure 5-3

therefore move faster than the particle passing along the lower surface.

A law of physics tells us that as air moves along a surface at increasing speed, sideways pressure decreases. Since the particle passing along the upper surface of the airfoil is traveling faster, pressure there is less. The result is a partial vacuum over the upper surface of the airfoil. This partial vacuum provides the lift that enables an airplane to fly and a sailboat to sail.

Consider the airplane wing again: slow-flying aircraft must have a great amount of curvature to their upper wing surface whereas fast-flying jet aircraft require little curvature.

The sailing comparison is that gentle winds (called light air) call for a great amount of curvature to develop lift or partial vacuum on the leeward (downwind) side of the sail (fig. 5–3). Conversely, strong winds (known as heavy air) call for a flatter sail with less curvature.

We can therefore conclude that in light air the sails should be relatively loosely trimmed for maximum curvature whereas in heavy air the sails should be trimmed flat to use less of the wind's force.

This airfoil, or draft, is basically built into the sail by the sailmaker. However, it can be altered somewhat by the lines, called running rigging, that raise the sails and control their shape.

Now look at a push-pull force made up of two components acting at right angles to each other, one toward the bow of the boat trying to drive it ahead, the other toward the lee side of the boat trying to drive it sideways (fig. 5–4).

To increase lateral resistance and decrease sideways movement (leeway), sailboats have a centerboard, fixed keel, or combination (fig. 1–13). The resistance of this large, flat plane to sideways movement is, of course, much greater than the resistance to forward movement. (A heavy keel or centerboard also increases stability, helping to keep the boat upright against the force of the wind on the sails.)

As a result of the forces acting on the sail and the resistance of the underbody, the boat moves

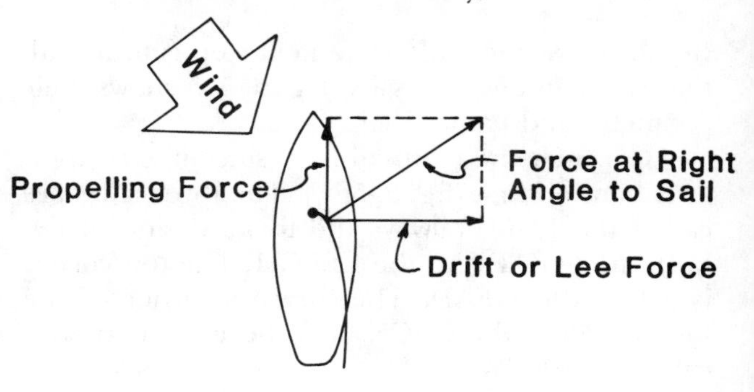

Effect of Wind Forces

Figure 5-4

forward; (makes headway) faster than it drifts downwind (makes leeway).

Running Rigging

Figure 1–3 shows the basic sailboat, without the sails in place. The rigging shown there is called standing rigging, not only because it permits the mast to stand and remain in place when sails are furled. It also supports the mast when loads from the wind forces are applied to the sails.

Let us assume at this point that our sailboat is in the water, on the leeward or downwind side of the dock. (Launching of the trailered sailboat is discussed in the section on BOAT TRAILERING.) Secure the boat to the dock only by the bow line, or painter, so as to permit it to swing as the wind shifts slightly. This is important because it permits the boat to be always bow-to-wind. First thing upon boarding the boat, lower the centerboard all the way. This diminishes the boat's tendency to heel and makes it easier for you to move around.

Bending On the Sails. The next step is to install, that is "bend on," the sails. Figure 5–5 shows their geometry and names their parts.

Consider the mainsail first, since it is customarily bent on first (fig. 5–5[b]). The three sides are called the LUFF (always the forward side of the sail), the FOOT, and the LEECH. The top corner is called the HEAD. The forward corner of the foot is called the TACK and the after corner is called the CLEW.

Install the foot first. It is secured to the boom with SAIL SLIDES, which fit over the sail track on the top surface of the boom. Starting with the clew end of the sail, install each sail side in sequence, taking care that all are facing the same way and are not twisted. The foot of the sail should lie smoothly along the boom. Pull the clew out to the after end if the boom for securing later. Next install the slides on the luff of the sail in the same fashion, pushing them up the mast track to make room for the next one. Then secure the tack to the gooseneck fitting. After the main has been bent on, insert the BATTENS in the batten pockets, thin edge forward. Now tie several light

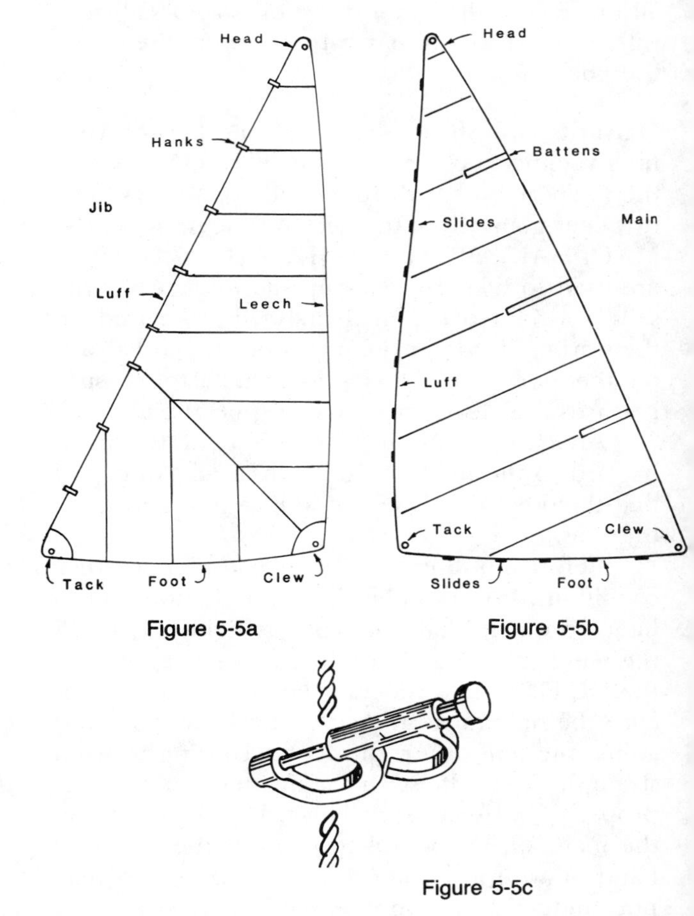

Figure 5-5a

Figure 5-5b

Figure 5-5c

lines, called sail stops, around the sail to keep it from thrashing about while the jib is bent on.

Notice that the jib (fig. 5–5[a]) has snap hooks called HANKS, (fig. 5–5[c]) instead of slides. These hanks hold the jib to the forestay. First locate the tack and shackle it to the tack fitting or stem fitting at the lower end of the forestay. Many sailmakers label the tack. Attach the hanks from bottom to top making sure again that all are facing the same direction so no sail twist will occur. If the jib has battens, insert them into the pockets.

Halyards and Sheets. Now it's time for the running rigging to come into play. Figure 5–6 shows the basic sailboat with some additional lines. The two lines going from the deck up the mast are the MAIN HALYARD and the JIB HALYARD. These are used to hoist the sails up the mast. After the sails are hoisted the main halyard is secured on the starboard side of the mast and the jib halyard on the port side. Always look aloft to be sure halyards are clear before hauling on them.

Attach the shackle at one end of the main halyard to the head of the mainsail, making sure that the other end is secure so it cannot escape up the mast.

Before hoisting the main, consider weather conditions. If the wind is light, you do not want to haul up on the halyard quite as tightly as when the wind is strong. The same concept applies to the OUTHAUL at the after end of the boom. Secure the outhaul to the clew of the mainsail and adjust the tension on the foot according to wind strength. Then hoist the main, tension the luff properly, and secure the halyard. (When hoisting the mainsail, be careful to support the boom by hand or with a topping lift. Otherwise, you may put undue strain on the leech and stretch it,

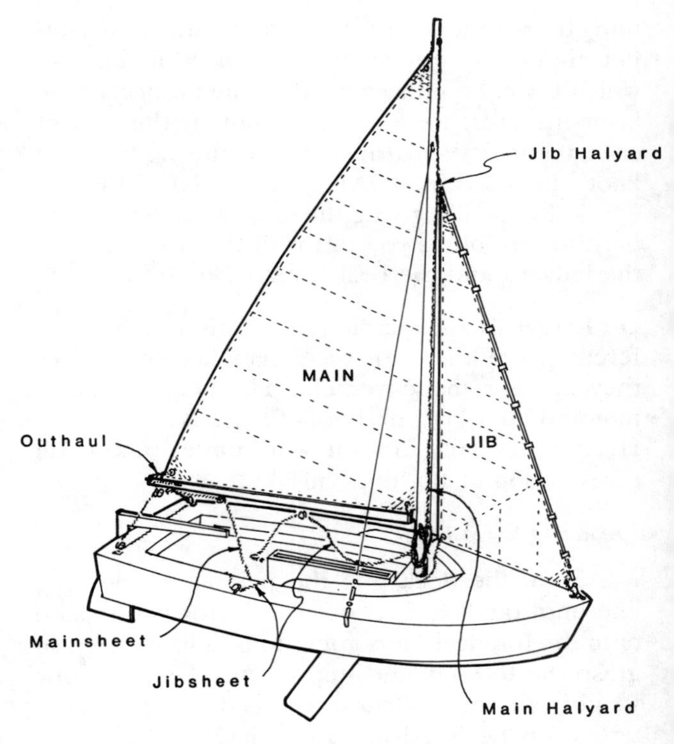

Jib Halyard on Port Side of Mast

Figure 5-6

damaging the sail.) Just get the excess halyard stowed out of the way for now. The proper way to coil lines is discussed at the end of this lesson.

Notice that there is a line running from the boom into the cockpit. This is the MAINSHEET, which is used to control the angle of the mainsail. This line goes through the pulleys, called mainsheet blocks, and is left loose in the cockpit, free to run.

Now let's look at the jib. In order to trim this sail, the JIBSHEETS must be attached to the clew. The best knot to use for this purpose is a bowline (discussed in ELEMENTARY SEAMANSHIP Section) because it is easy to tie and untie and does not tighten-up under the considerable load to which it will be subjected. After the jibsheets have been installed, tie a stopper knot in the end of each to hold them captive. Use the figure-eight knot (discussed in BOAT TYPES AND TERMS.)

Raise the jib, giving the same consideration to halyard tension as you did with the main. Secure the halyard and the boat is ready to go for a sail.

On Larger Boats. Bending on sails is a slightly different procedure with the larger keelboats since they are less maneuverable. The boat is usually motored out of the harbor before sails are hoisted. Heading the boat into the wind under power will ease the job of hoisting sails.

Preparing to Cast Off

From the dock pull the painter or mooring line until the boat is close enough for you to step onto the foredeck. It is going to be a little tippy, so grasp the forestay and step aboard, keeping your weight as low as practical. Proceed along the centerline of the foredeck to the mast and step into the cockpit.

See that the centerboard is all the way down. Make sure that the rudder is securely installed and locked in place and that the arc through which the tiller will swing is unobstructed. Be certain that the mainsheet and jibsheets are correctly positioned and that they are free to run through their blocks with no kinks in the lines. Ensure that you have enough life preservers aboard; if wind conditions warrant, put one on and require that your crew do the same.

Stow any required equipment not immediately needed in an accessible, out-of-the-way place. Make sure that the halyards are properly coiled and stowed.

When all this has been accomplished, you are ready for the rest of the crew to board. Have them come aboard as you did and use your weight to counteract their tendency to heel the boat. Position the crew so that their weight is as evenly distributed as possible from side to side along the middle third of the boat.

Before getting underway, determine your initial point of sail by studying Figure 5–7.

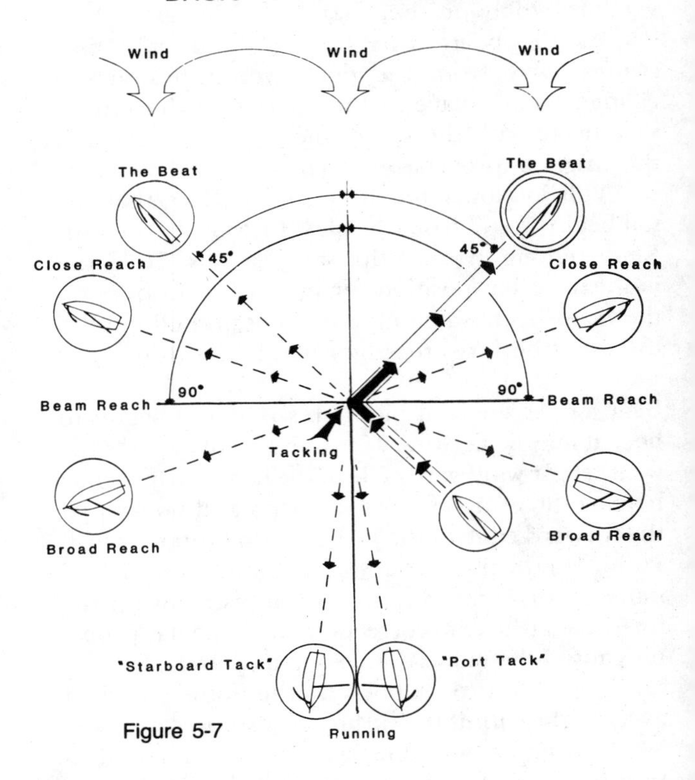

Figure 5-7

Leaving the Dock

If there is someone on the dock who can help, you can depart with little effort on the part of the crew. Have the person on the dock untie the mooring line, throw it aboard, and give the bow a good shove backward and away from the dock. At the same time, push the tiller down to leeward. This will help swing the bow away from the dock and to leeward. If no one is on the dock, one of the crew will have to go forward to shove off and bring the mooring line aboard. The crew should stay as low as possible during this maneuver, preferably on their hands and knees.

As the boat drifts backward and the bow swings away from the dock, you will notice a change taking place in the angle that the luffing sails make with the centerline of the boat. When this angle approaches 45°, you can start sailing.

Pull in slowly on the jibsheet. Note that the sail begins to fill from the clew forward to the luff. Keep pulling-in until the sail just fills. Hold the jibsheet in that position for now. Pull in slowly on the mainsheet, watching the mainsail. Pull in until the luff (the forward edge) is full and drawing.

Beating. As the boat picks up speed and begins to heel, it may be necessary for the crew to move to the weather, or windward, side of the boat to counteract heeling. Steer up close to the wind and notice that the forward edge of the jib begins to flutter, or luff. Pull-in on the jibsheet until the fluttering stops and make a corresponding inward adjustment on the mainsheet (the trim correction on the jib has probably caused the mainsail to begin to flutter). If hauling in the sheet does not stop the fluttering, steer away slightly until the luffing just stops.

You are now sailing as close to the wind as possible. You are said to be sailing *close-hauled* (fig. 5–7), or *beating* into the wind. Your position is about 45° off the true wind. Although some boats may sail somewhat higher, or closer to the wind, this is a good average for the modern sailboat.

If the wind is coming over the starboard side of the boat, you are beating on a starboard tack.

You can continue on this tack as long as you like or until you run out of sailing room. But sooner or later you will have to return to your point of departure using the other points of sail.

Tacking. You can change direction by *tacking* (fig. 5–8). Tacking is generally defined as going from a beat with the wind on one side of the boat to a beat with the wind on the other side (fig. 5–9). You are now sailing on a starboard tack, so you will bring the bow of the boat up toward the wind direction and through it until the wind strikes the port side of the boat. The jib will change sides sometime about the middle of this maneuver, so the sheet that the crew has been holding will have to be slacked and the sheet on the other side will become the working sheet. The boom will also change from slightly to port of the centerline to slightly to starboard. This will happen faster than the jib changes over, so be ready to duck.

Before beginning the tack, check to see that the jibsheets and mainsheet are free to run and that all unnecessary gear is out of the way. The crew should be ready to shift sides of the boat: on the new tack, the boat will heel in the opposite direction and the port side will be the high side. Make sure that you have room to tack without hitting another boat.

The skipper alerts the crew of his intention to tack by saying "Ready about" (or "Ready to come about?"). The crew gets ready and responds "Ready."

When the skipper is satisfied, he says "Hard alee" (or "Helms alee" or "Coming about") and smoothly pushes the tiller well down to leeward.

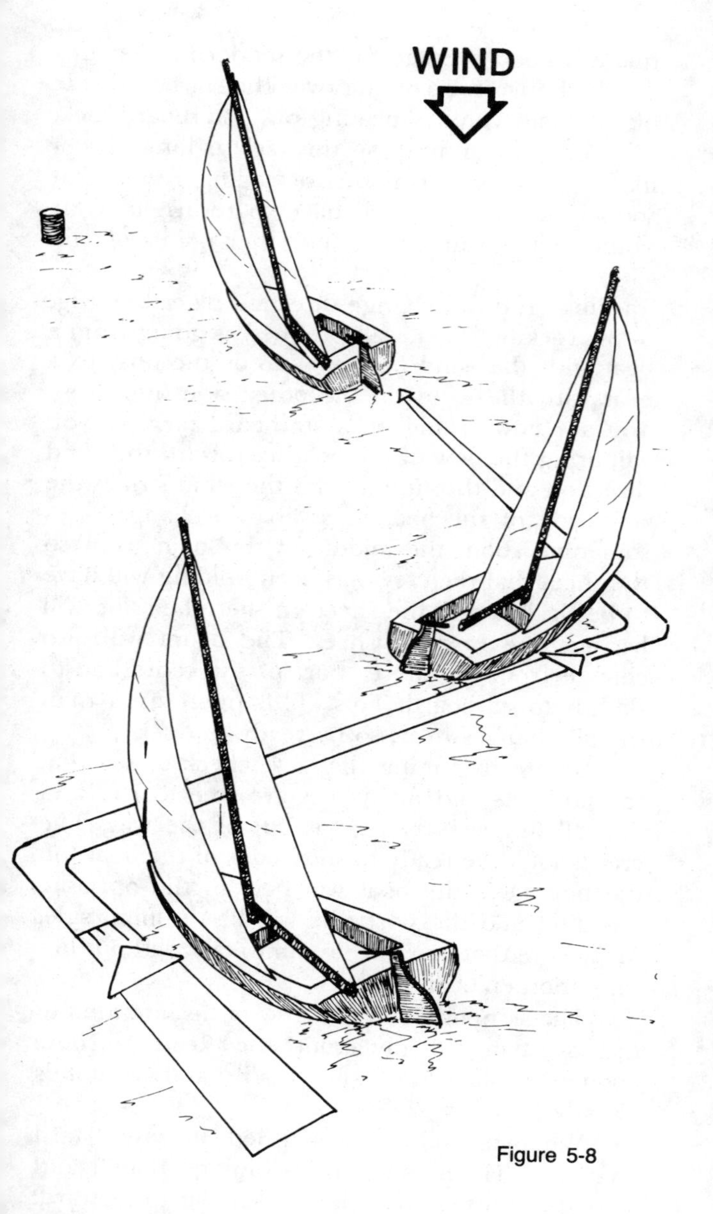

Figure 5-8

As soon as the jib breaks and begins to luff, the crew releases the port side jibsheet and watches to see that it runs smoothly through the block. While doing this, the crew pulls in the starboard jibsheet and changes position to the port side of the boat. The skipper ducks under the boom as it comes across and positions himself on the port side after releasing the mainsail slightly as it begins to luff. The crew, meanwhile, trims in the jib to about the same distance from the centerline as on the other tack. Bring the boat up into the wind and when the jib just starts to luff, fall away slightly while trimming in on the mainsheet until the main just stops luffing. You are now correctly trimmed on a *port tack.*

As the boat picks up speed, ease up into the wind again and attempt to take-in slightly on the jib to see if the boat is as close to the wind as it can go. If you sail too close to the wind, the sail will stall just as an airplane wing stalls; the pressure differential between the windward and leeward sides of the sail will drop and the boat will slow down.

Sailing as close to the wind as possible without stalling (sailors often say "pinching"), you are beating, or sailing close-hauled.

Reaching. Now let's explore the other points of sail shown in figure 5–7. If you ease the jib a foot or so, let out the mainsail a bit, and steer slightly away from the wind, all the while checking to see that both sails just fill without luffing on this new course, you are on a *reach.* This point of sail is called a close reach because the wind, as observed from the boat, is forward of the beam (fig. 5–7).

Always remember to change sail trim as you change course, according to this rule: *First trim the jib, then trim the main.*

Steer a bit farther away from the wind (be sure to adjust your sails) until the wind as observed from the boat is abeam. Now you are on a beam reach. The experienced sailor would say

Figure 5-9

that you have "fallen off the wind," or "fallen down." Sailors customarily use "up" to mean toward or closer to the wind and "down" or "off" to mean away from the wind.

("Wind" as used here is not the *true wind* you feel when standing still on shore but the *apparent wind* you actually experience on a moving boat. It's important to understand that apparent wind is a combination of the true wind and the so-called wind you would feel just from the movement of the boat. *Your boat sails in the apparent wind.* You will find that the apparent wind—which is always from somewhere between the true wind and the bow of your boat—seems stronger than the true wind when forward of the beam, weaker than the true wind when abaft the beam.)

Using the sailor's terminology, let's fall off some more until the wind is aft of the beam, say across the quarter of the boat. You are now on a broad reach.

Running. This is sailing with the wind astern. Falling off until the wind is dead behind the boat will cause the jib to collapse because of being blanketed or screened by the mainsail. But the jib can be pulled over to the other side of the boat and trimmed from that side. This is called sailing "wing and wing."

In falling off the wind, you probably noticed that the boat showed less and less tendency to heel. When the wind is farther aft, there is less sideways force on the sails and less need for the action of the centerboard. Therefore, it should be progressively hoisted as you alter course to leeward. When you head dead downwind, it should be all the way up.

Jibing. Be aware that sailing dead downwind can be dangerous. If the wind changes direction, or

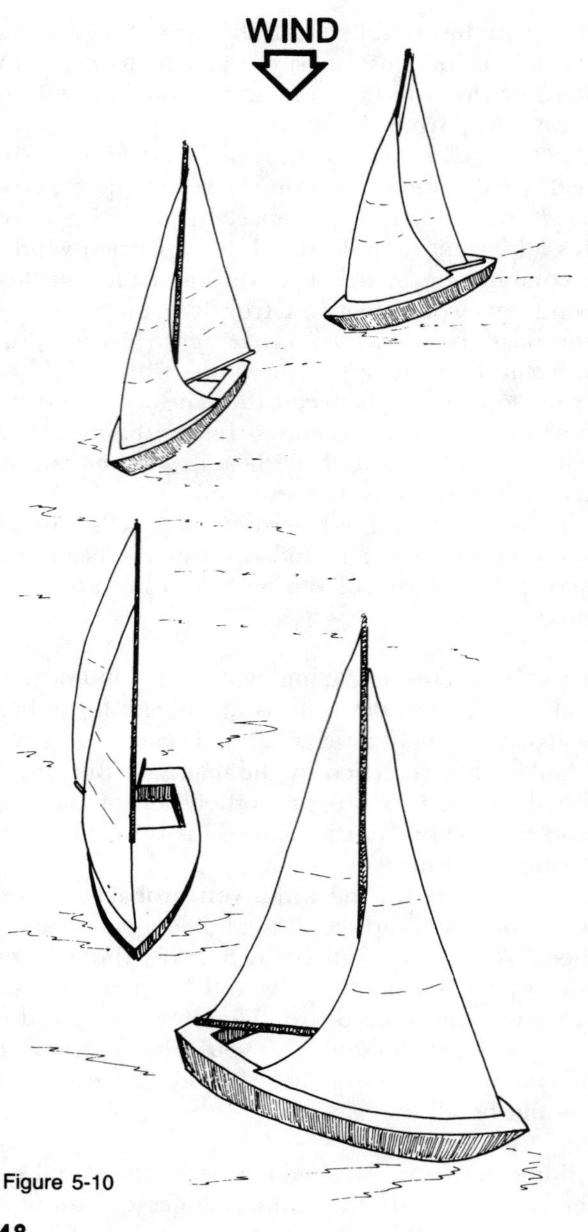

Figure 5-10

the wake from a powerboat running too close slues your boat around, the wind may get *behind* the mainsail. The sail will swing abruptly, and sometimes violently, to the other side of the boat. This is called an accidental jibe. A boom swinging at full speed can damage fittings and the boom itself, or even break a stay and cause a dismasting. Furthermore, it can seriously injure you or a member of the crew.

Sometimes, however, you must intentionally jibe the boat (fig. 5–10). To do this, haul in the mainsheet while sailing dead downwind. Then, as the boom approaches the centerline of the boat, quickly change course until the wind is on the other side of the sail. Now ease out on the mainsheet until the sail is properly set and the jib is adjusted to the new course. *This time you trim the main before trimming the jib.*

Having successfully jibed the boat, you can now head back toward the dock.

Remember, when you were sailing downwind you had the centerboard pulled all the way up. Now as you sail up closer to the wind, you must continually lower the board until it is all the way down again when back on a beat. In beating or reaching, the large, flat plane of the centerboard increases lateral resistance and reduces sideways movement (leeway).

Returning to the Dock

One thing you learned in tacking is that the boat must have enough momentum to follow through the tack to your new point of sail. This momentum, often called "way" by sailors, varies with the speed and weight of the boat. Way is also affected by the sea surface and the amount of hull surface presented to the wind when heading into it.

You can learn how to use way to bring the boat up to the dock, just close enough to lay a line around a cleat or post without hitting the dock.

To do it right and earn the respect of other sailors—as well as to avoid damaging your boat—practice the maneuver away from the dock.

Practice Docking. Select an object in the water as a mark—for example, a buoy, a fishing marker, a life preserver—and practice approaching it (fig. 5–11). Remember to lower your centerboard to increase maneuverability and reduce leeway. Use the points of sail shown in fig. 5–7. From downwind, head past the mark on a reach and estimate how much way the boat has. A little before you are abeam of the mark, come up to a beat. When you are directly downwind of the mark, head into the wind with your sails luffing and see how close you come to the mark.

If you can just put a line on the mark, you would have made a good landing at the dock. If you go past the mark, you would have hit the dock. If you fall short, you would have had to sail out and try again.

When all way is lost, the boat becomes dead in the water—bow to the wind, sails luffing, and steering lost. This is called being "in irons," or "caught in stays." Shortly the boat will begin to drift downwind owing to the windage of the hull and rig. As the boat gathers sternway, notice which side of the bow is falling away from the wind and put the tiller over to that side to help. This maneuver—getting out of irons—is not unlike the one used to leave the dock. To help swing the bow, hold the jib out toward the side of the boat nearest the wind (backwind the jib). As in leaving the dock, when the bow is about 45° off the wind, trim and sails and sail off.

If necessary, practice approaching a mark

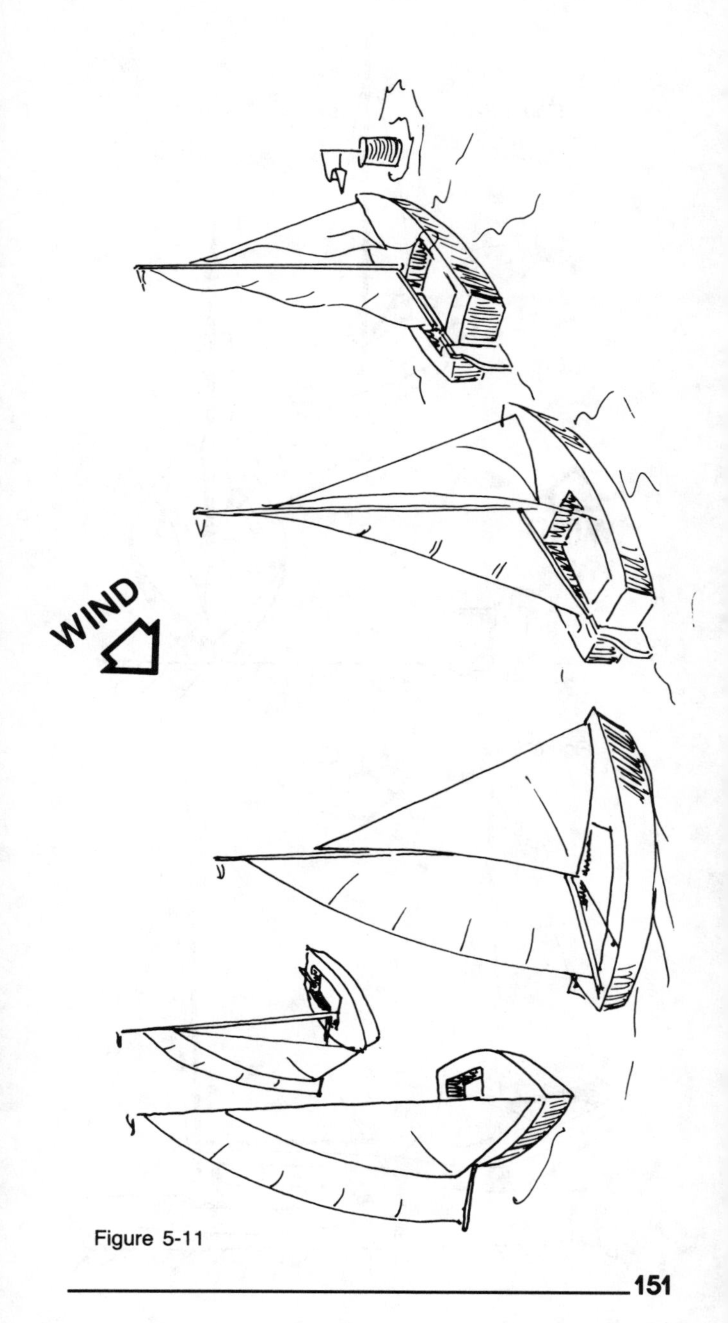

Figure 5-11

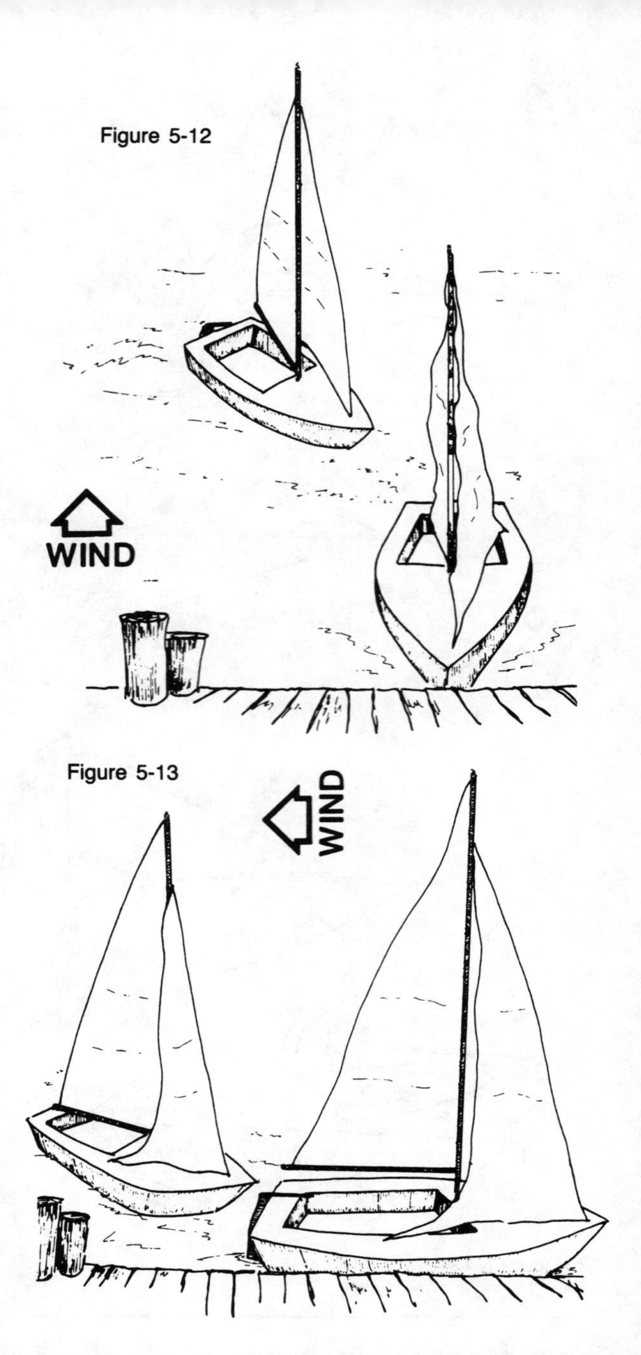

Figure 5-12

Figure 5-13

again and again until you can accurately estimate the boat's way. (This exercise may also be valuable one day in retrieving a man overboard.)

Now is the time to practice with the real dock, as illustrated in figures 5–12, 5–13, and 5–14.

Wind From Dock. Prepare the boat for docking by putting fenders over the side and readying lines. Sail toward the dock, making sure of the wind direction. (Note the heading of boats hanging off the leeward side of the dock; this will be your final heading as you shoot into the wind for your landing.) As you approach the dock (fig. 5–12), select a landing place and come up onto a beat just before you are downwind of the spot. At the right time, head directly into the wind.

If you have practiced well, you will arrive at the dock just as you lose way.

A member of the crew should be on the bow with the painter in hand to place it over a cleat or to toss it to someone on the dock. Never permit the crew to fend off with hands or feet. Broken gear is a lot less painful than broken bones. If your estimate of carry is a bit on the conservative side, grab onto an adjacent boat and pull your boat up to the dock.

Belay the painter to a cleat or pile. Drop the sails.

Wind Parallel to Dock. If the wind is blowing along the dock (fig. 5–13), make your approach on a beam reach. Allow the sails to luff a bit if you need to reduce speed. As you near the dock, turn into the wind. The boat's way should bring you alongside.

Wind Onto Dock. This situation (fig. 5–14) calls for special caution to keep the wind from smashing your boat into the dock, or the boom into a

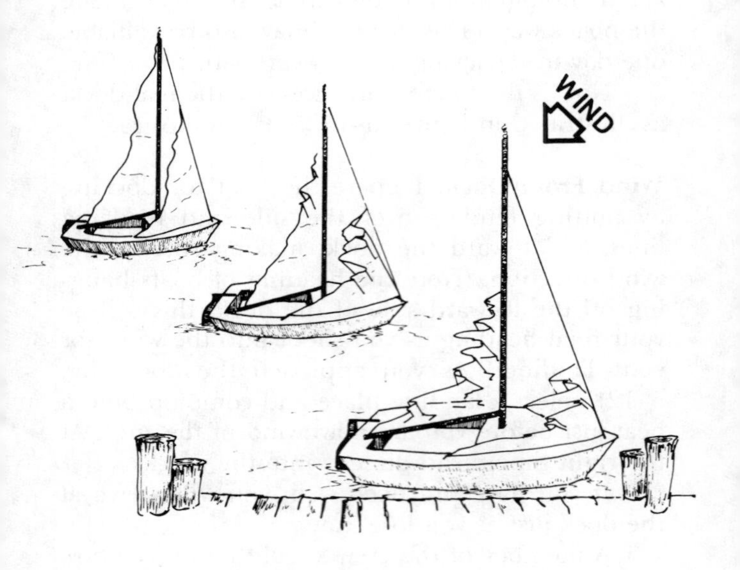

Figure 5-14

piling. In light air—no more than that—head up and drop the sails. Then let the wind bring you in broadside to the dock. In strong winds, set an anchor upwind and use the rode to ease the boat down to the dock.

Docking Larger Boats. If you have a larger boat, head it into the wind and drop the sails. Secure them and return to the dock under power. However, you should practice the maneuvers described here—they are valuable in developing boat-handling experience.

Section 5: STUDY QUESTIONS FOR SAILING

1. You have just boarded your centerboard sailboat at the dock. The first thing you should do is:
   (a) attach the rudder.
   (b) bend on the mainsail.
   (c) check to see that the centerboard is all the way down.
   (d) make sure that the boat is on the windward side of the dock.

2. You are bending on the jib. The corner you attach first is:
   (a) the clew.
   (b) the head.
   (c) the foot.
   (d) the tack.

3. If your sailboat has a centerboard, the purpose is to:
   (a) strike sandbars or rocks on the bottom before the hull hits.
   (b) provide a large, flat surface to reduce sideways movement of the boat (leeway).
   (c) keep the boat going in a straight line.
   (d) make the boat go faster.

4. You are about to raise the sails on your sloop and have observed that the winds are strong. You decide that your halyard tension should be:
   (a) very tight on both main and jib.
   (b) slacked off an inch or so on both main and jib.
   (c) tight on the main and slacked on the jib.
   (d) slacked on the main and tight on the jib.

5. When sailing your boat as nearly into the wind as possible, you are:

   (a) running.
   (b) on a beam reach.
   (c) beating.
   (d) on a broad reach.

6. When a sailboat becomes dead in the water, bow to the wind and sails luffing, it is said to be "in irons." To get out of irons, you would:

   (a) wait until the wind shifts and refills the sails.
   (b) put the tiller over toward the side opposite that to which the bow is drifting.
   (c) hold the mainsail to the side toward the wind.
   (d) put the tiller over toward the side to which the bow is drifting and hold the jib to the side toward the wind.

7. You are beating to weather in your boat. Your centerboard should be:

   (a) halfway down.
   (b) all the way down.
   (c) all the way up.
   (d) three fourths of the way down.

8. When sailing a small boat downwind, or running, you should:

   (a) be prepared for a jibe, when the boom swings from one side to the other.
   (b) watch for wakes of powerboats running too close, which can cause a jibe.
   (c) keep the wind a few degrees to port or starboard of dead aft so as to avoid a jibe.
   (d) all of the above.

9. The wind is forward of the beam and you alter course slightly to weather, causing both sails to luff. Which sail should you trim first?

   (a) It doesn't make any difference.
   (b) Trim them both at the same time.
   (c) Trim the main, then the jib.
   (d) Trim the jib, then the main.

10. You go out with a friend in his 18-foot sailboat. After a pleasant sail you head for the dock. You notice that he approaches the dock:

    (a) with the wind behind him.
    (b) on a close reach.
    (c) into the wind.
    (d) with the sails down.

11. When approaching a mooring out in the water, you should:

    (a) sail close by on a run and grab the thing as you go by.
    (b) approach the mooring on a beat and then shoot into the wind to reach it.
    (c) sail up to it on a broad reach and throw a line over it.
    (d) go upwind and drift down to it.

12. You are ready to cast off in your sailboat, intending to sail to a dock that bears 010° true from you. The wind is from the north. You realize that in order to get there, you will have to sail:

    (a) a course of 010° True.
    (b) first on a course of 090° True, then 335° True to the dock.
    (c) alternate courses of 045° True and 315° True to the dock.
    (d) somewhere else, as you can't get there from here.

SECTION 6

Navigation Rules, Marine Radiotelephone, and Boat Trailering

NAVIGATION RULES

The primary purpose of the Navigation Rules is to prevent collision on the water. These Rules are regulations that have the force of law. They prescribe how you are to pilot your boat in the presence of others, and how you are to inform others of your presence and intentions.

The best time to know the Rules (and the worst time to study them) is when a collision is imminent.

ABOUT THE RULES

To unify, consolidate, and modernize our rules governing navigation, recent legislation limits them to just two sets: *Inland Navigation Rules,* which apply to all vessels on the inland waters of the United States; and *International Navigation Rules,* which apply to all vessels on the high seas. These two sets agree in basic principles. In Canada, these rules are covered in the "Collision Regulations."

Since we could never devise rules that would cover every possible risk of collision, we also have "Rules of Good Seamanship" and the "General

Prudential Rule." These rules state that attention shall be given to all hazards of navigation, threats of collision, or special circumstances that may require a departure from the customary procedures to avoid immediate danger.

In other words, common sense must always accompany the application of the Navigation Rules, and you must do everything you can to avoid a collision, even if it involves breaking the rules. Collision indicates that both parties are at fault, regardless of who had the right-of-way.

Navigation Rules are designated as either Inland, International, or both. In this section, when the statement includes "the Rules," the rule applies to both.

STEERING AND SAILING RULES

Except where specifically required otherwise, power-driven vessels under way must keep out of the way of:

(a) a vessel not under command (unable to maneuver as required and therefore unable to keep out of the way of another vessel);
(b) a vessel restricted in her ability to maneuver;
(c) a vessel engaged in fishing; and
(d) a sailing vessel.

Sailing vessels must keep out of the way of (a), (b), and (c). Vessels engaged in fishing must keep out of the way of (a) and (b).

Right-of-Way

There are three close-approach situations involving risk of collision that you must understand:

OVERTAKING, MEETING, and CROSSING. These may be collectively referred to as "passing situations." What you do depends on the kind of boat you are operating, where you are in relation to the other boat, and conditions of visibility.

ALL VESSELS

Overtaking

Any vessel (including a sailboat) overtaking any other must keep out of the way of the vessel being overtaken (fig. 6–1). A vessel is overtaking when coming up to another vessel from a direction more than 22.5 degrees abaft (behind) her beam. At night, the overtaking vessel would be able to see the stern light of the overtaken vessel, but neither of her sidelights.

In Inland waters, an overtaking power-driven vessel may not pass until she gives the proper

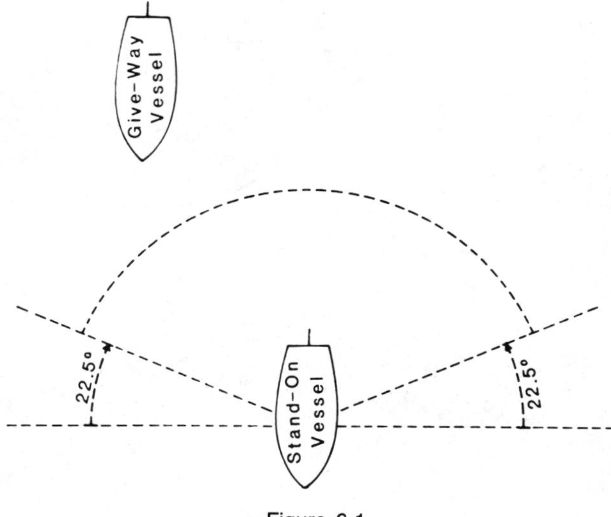

Figure 6-1

sound signals and they are answered by the vessel being overtaken.

SAILING VESSELS

When two sailing vessels approach one another so as to involve risk of collision, one of them must keep out of the way of the other as follows:

- (a) When each has the wind on a different side, the vessel that has the wind on the port (left) side must keep out of the way of the other (fig. 6–2).
- (b) When both have the wind on the same side, the vessel that is to windward must keep out of the way of the vessel to leeward (fig. 6–3).
- (c) If a vessel with the wind on the port side sees a vessel to windward and cannot be sure whether the other vessel has the

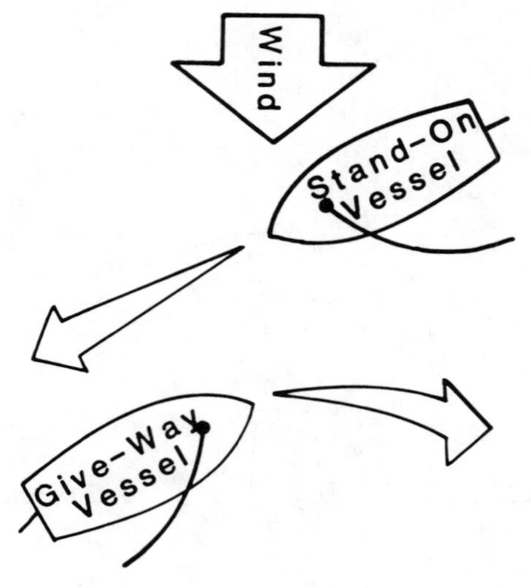

Figure 6-2

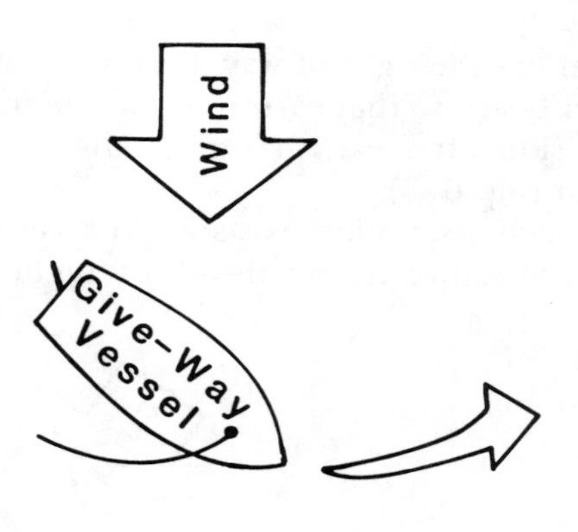

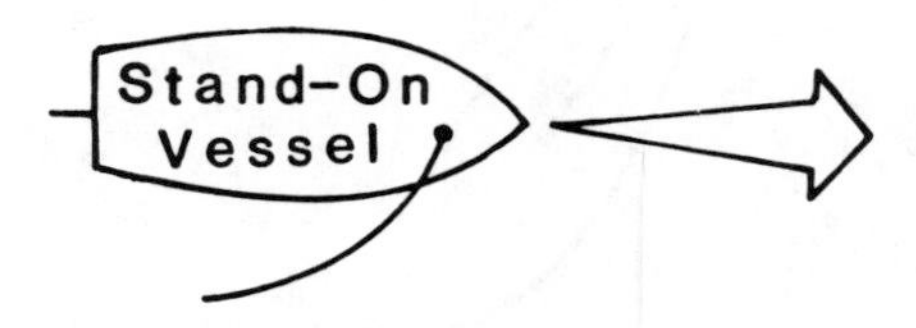

Figure 6-3

wind on the port or on the starboard side, she must keep out of the way of the other vessel (fig. 6–4).

The windward side is the side opposite that on which the mainsail is carried.

As a practical matter, all small boats should keep out of the way of large, less maneuverable vessels.

POWER-DRIVEN VESSELS

Meeting Head on

When two power-driven vessels are meeting head on so as to involve risk of collision, neither vessel has the right-of-way. Each must alter course to starboard so that each will pass the other on the port side, after each has given the proper sound signal (fig. 6–5).

Such a situation exists when a vessel sees the other ahead or nearly ahead. By night, she could

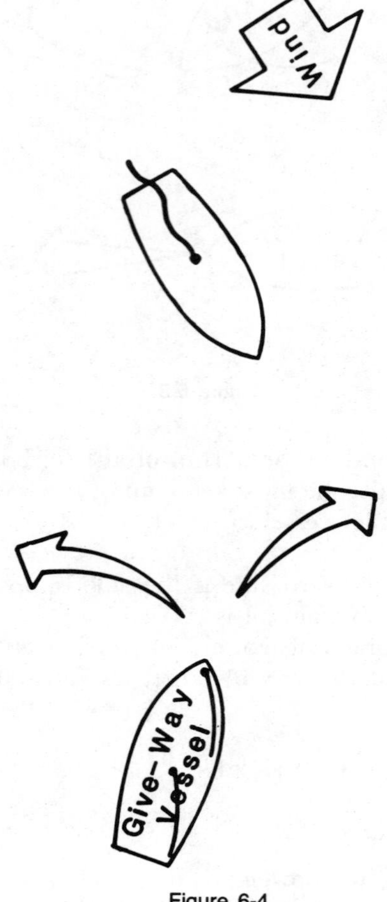

Figure 6-4

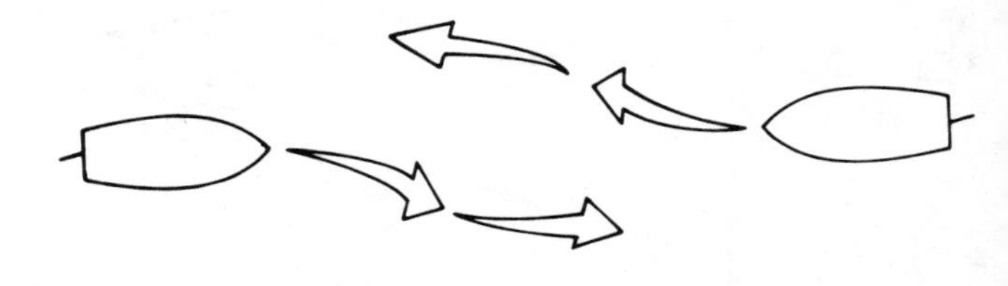

Figure 6-5

see the masthead light and both sidelights of the other.

Crossing

When two power-driven vessels are crossing so as to involve risk of collision, the vessel that has the other on her starboard (right) side is the give-way vessel and must keep out of the way of the other. The give-way vessel must take early and substantial action to keep well clear. The other vessel is the stand-on vessel, and she must hold her course and speed. The stand-on vessel *may,* however, take action to avoid collision by her maneuver alone as soon as it becomes apparent that the give-way vessel is not taking appropriate action in compliance with these rules, and MUST take action if it appears that collision cannot otherwise be avoided.

If a vessel is coming up to another vessel from a line 22.5 degrees abaft the beam of the vessel being approached, the situation is considered an OVERTAKING one. If, however, vessels approach each other forward of 22.5 degrees abaft the beam, the situation is considered a CROSSING one (fig. 6–6).

Risk of collision can be gauged by carefully watching the relative bearing of an approaching vessel. If the bearing does not change appreciably,

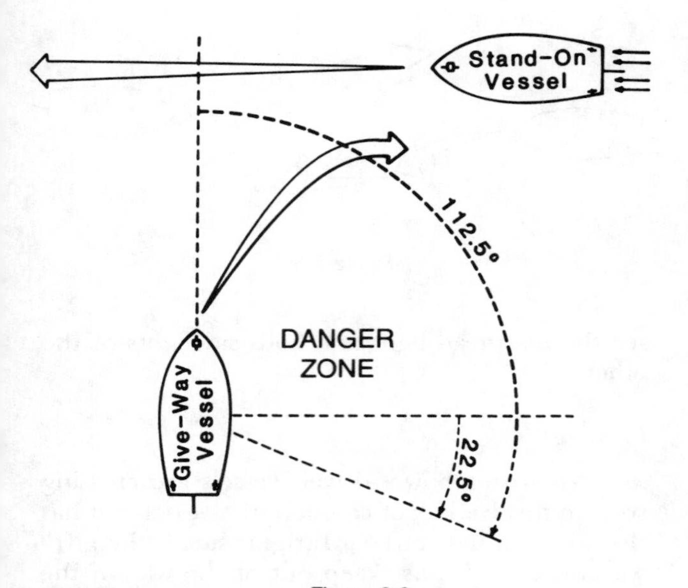

Figure 6-6

it indicates that the vessels are on a collision course.

MANEUVERING, WARNING SIGNALS

Sound signals used in passing or crossing situations in Inland waters require a "signal of intent" from the vessel first indicating her intended motion, and then a "signal of consent" from the other vessel. In International waters, only a signal of "action taken" is given, and no answering signal. (A vessel may supplement the sound signals with light signals synchronized with the sound.)

These sound signals are *not* to be used under conditions of restricted visibility unless the vessels are in sight of each other.

When power-driven vessels are in sight of one another and MEETING or CROSSING within half a mile of each other, each vessel must indicate her maneuver by the following signals on her whistle (horn):

One short blast means "I intend to leave (pass) you on my port side" (fig. 6–7). The Rules specifically require that if two power-driven vessels are meeting head on, or nearly so, each is to alter course to starboard so as to pass port side to port side.

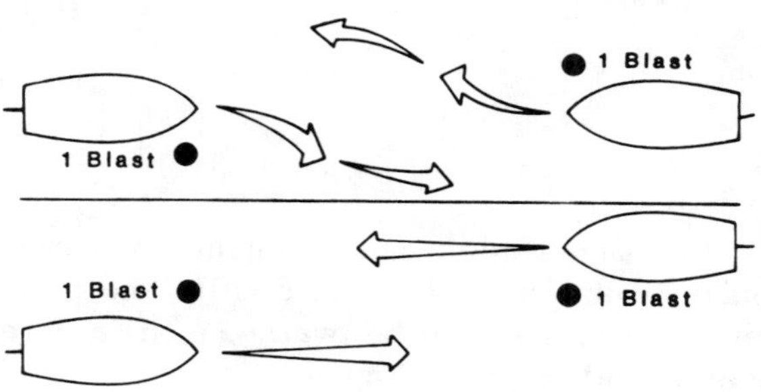

Figure 6-7

Two short blasts mean "I intend to leave you on my starboard side" (fig. 6–8).

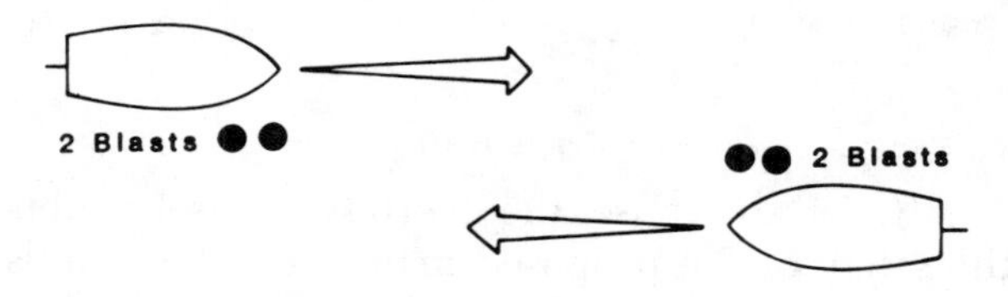

Figure 6-8

On hearing the one-blast or two-blast signal, the other vessel, if in agreement, must sound the same whistle signal and take steps to affect a safe passing. No vessel may use "cross signals"—that is, answer one blast with two, or two blasts with one.

A power-driven vessel OVERTAKING another power-driven vessel must indicate her intention by the following signals:

One short blast means "I intend to overtake you on your starboard side" (fig. 6–9). The power-driven vessel about to be overtaken, if in agreement, sounds a similar signal.

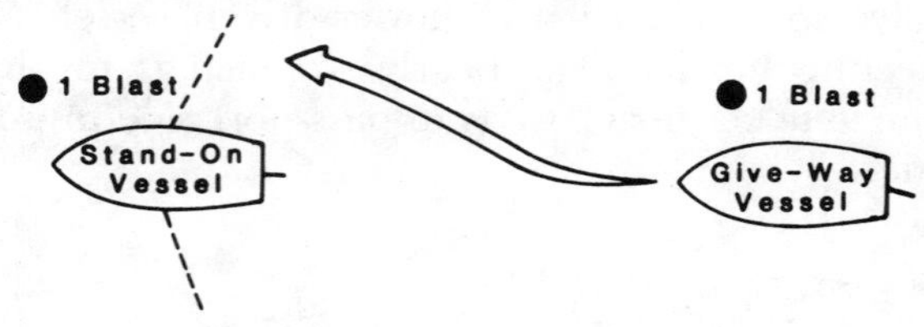

Figure 6-9

Two short blasts mean "I intend to overtake you on your port side" (fig. 6–10). The power-driven vessel about to be overtaken, if in agreement, sounds a similar signal.

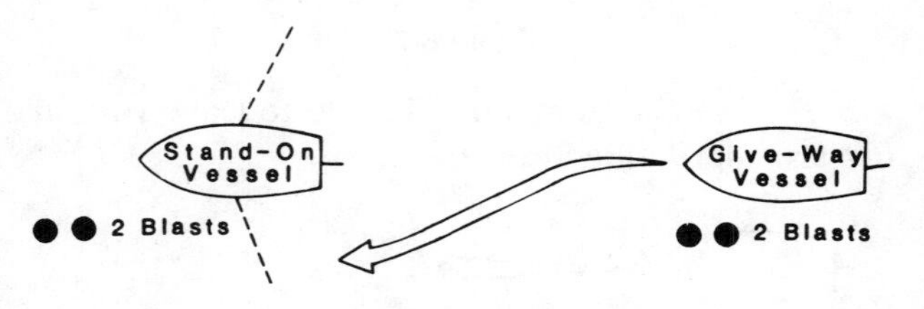

Figure 6-10

If, for any cause, the overtaken vessel doubts the safety of the proposed maneuver, she sounds the *danger signal* of at least *five short, rapid blasts.* Then, each vessel must take precautionary action until a safe passing agreement is reached.

Three short blasts mean "I am operating astern propulsion" (backing down). Vessel may not actually be moving astern.

One long blast means "I am leaving my berth."

Sound signals are *not* exchanged between power-driven vessels and sailing vessels, nor between sailing vessels under sail only.

RESTRICTED VISIBILITY

When visibility is restricted by fog, haze, snow, heavy rain, sandstorms, and other causes, a vessel must slow down and proceed with caution. Navigation lights must be displayed and proper sound signals given.

Sound Signals

A vessel that hears, forward of her beam, the fog signal of another vessel, or cannot avoid a close-quarter situation with another vessel forward of her beam, must reduce speed to the minimum at which she can stay on course. Or, if necessary, she must take off all way and navigate with extreme caution until danger of collision is over. *A good rule of thumb is to hold to a speed that will allow you to stop in half the distance of visibility.*

A power-driven vessel under way must sound one prolonged blast at least every 2 minutes. A power-driven vessel under way, but stopped and making no way through the water, must sound two prolonged blasts in succession, with an interval of about 2 seconds between them, every 2 minutes.

A sailing vessel under way must sound three blasts in succession—one prolonged blast and two short blasts—at intervals of not more than 2 minutes. This also applies to a vessel not under command; a vessel restricted in her ability to maneuver, whether under way or at anchor; and a vessel engaged in towing or pushing another vessel.

Vessel at Anchor

The sound signal required of a vessel at anchor when visibility is restricted depends on her size. A vessel 12 meters (39 ft. 4 in.) or longer must ring a bell rapidly for about 5 seconds at intervals of not more than 1 minute. A vessel under 12 meters long need not give this signal but, if she does not, she must make some other efficient sound signal at intervals of not more than 2 minutes. A vessel at anchor *may,* in addition, sound three blasts in succession—one short, one prolonged, and one short—to warn others of her position.

When at anchor in a special anchorage area, a vessel under 20 meters (65 ft. 6 in.) long need *not* sound these special signals or display an anchor light.

GENERAL COMMENTS

A self-propelled vessel 12 meters (39 ft. 4 in.) or longer must carry on board and maintain for ready reference a copy of the Inland Navigation Rules. (International Rules have no such requirement.)

When a vessel proceeds along a narrow fairway (channel), she must keep as near to the starboard side as is safe and practical.

The passage of a vessel that can safely navigate only within the narrow fairway must not be impeded by a vessel less than 20 meters (65 ft. 6 in.) long, a sailing vessel, or a vessel engaged in fishing.

A power-driven vessel operating in a narrow channel on the Great Lakes or the Western Rivers and proceeding downbound (downstream) with a following current has the right-of-way over an upbound (upstream) vessel.

Penalties

For violation of the Rules or related regulations, a civil penalty of as much as $5,000 may be levied against an operator for each violation. Also, the vessel is subject to the same penalty and may be seized and proceeded against in U.S. District Court.

Note

The Coast Guard has repeatedly asked for understanding from small craft operators in solving a long-standing problem: Recreational vessel owners continue to risk their vessels and their lives by refusing to give way to large commercial vessels. Operators of small craft must recognize that large vessels are usually limited in maneuverability. Operating small craft in the main shipping channels requires constant vigilance and should be avoided.

NAVIGATION LIGHTS

The headlights on your car are to help you see what lies ahead. A vessel's navigation lights (white, red, green, yellow, and blue) are to alert the other vessel to your presence, action, type, and size. (A vessel towing astern, alongside, or pushing ahead, or an air-cushioned vessel, displays a yellow light.)

Masthead Light

A white light placed over the fore and aft center line of the vessel, showing an unbroken light over an arc of the horizon of 225 degrees and so fixed as to show the light from dead ahead to 22.5 degrees abaft the beam on either side of the vessel.

Sidelight

A green light on the starboard side and a red

light on the port side of the vessel, each showing an unbroken light over an arc of the horizon of 112.5 degrees and so fixed as to show the light from dead ahead to 22.5 degrees abaft the respective beam. On a vessel of less than 20 meters (65 ft. 6 in.) long the sidelights may be combined in one lantern carried on the fore and aft center line of the vessel.

Stern Light

A white light placed as near as is practicable to the stern, showing an unbroken light over an arc of the horizon of 135 degrees and so fixed as to show the light 67.5 degrees aft on each side of the vessel.

All-round Light

A light showing an unbroken light over an arc of the horizon of 360 degrees.

Study these lights (fig. 6–11) and their angular ranges of visibility. If another vessel's colored lights and her white lights are visible, she must be approaching you head on!

If only her green sidelight, and her all-round white light are visible, she must be on a heading that permits you to see only her starboard side. She must be approaching your course line from your left. If the other vessel's red and white lights are visible to you off your bow, she is crossing from your starboard to your port. She is, therefore, in your "danger zone." She is the stand-on vessel and you are the give-way vessel.

Be extremely careful if only a white light is visible: you are either coming up behind a vessel moving in the same direction, or the other vessel is at anchor.

These navigation lights are to be displayed from sunset to sunrise, and you must not show

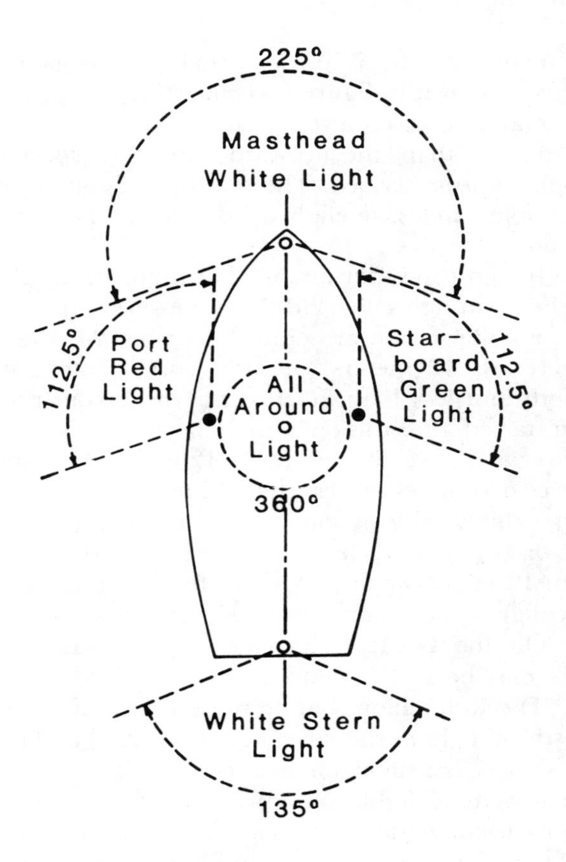

Figure 6-11

any other light that may be mistaken for them or impair their visibility. These lights are also to be displayed from sunrise to sunset if visibility is restricted and may be shown in other circumstances when necessary to improve the visibility of your boat.

Required Lights and Their Visibility

Required navigation lights on power-driven vessels differ slightly between the International and Inland Rules. A power-driven vessel less than

20 meters (65 ft. 7 in.) shall exhibit navigation lights as shown in figure 6–12 (a), (b), or (c). Options (a) and (b) require the aft masthead light to be higher than the forward one and specific heights are prescribed. The masthead lights must be visible 3 miles; sidelights and stern lights visible 2 miles.

Inland Rules permit an all-around white light as shown in figure 6–12(d) if the vessel's construction was started on or before December 24, 1981. All vessels 12 meters (39 ft. 4 in.) or more in length and less than 20 meters, whose construction started after this date, shall display navigation lights as shown in figure 6–12(a), (b), or (c). Power-driven vessels less than 12 meters in length may exhibit lights as shown in figure 6–12(a), (b), (c), or (d). The visibility of lights on vessels less than 12 meters shall be 2 miles for masthead and sternlights and 1 mile for sidelights.

On the Great Lakes, the second masthead light may be an all-round light.

The Rules allow, but do not require, the after masthead light as shown in figure 6–12 (a) and (b) on vessels less than 50 meters (164 ft.). Consequently, these light configurations are not commonly used. A sailing vessel under sail only and less than 20 meters (65 ft. 7 in.) long must display sidelights and a sternlight visible for 2 miles. Inland rules permit a combination of sternlight and sidelights in one lantern carried at or near the top of the mast where it can best be seen as shown in figure 6–13. International rules permit this triple fixture too, but only if the vessel is under 12 meters (39 ft. 4 in.) long.

A sailing vessel under sail only and less than 20 meters long *may* display, in addition to the sidelights and sternlight prescribed above, two all-round lights in a vertical line, the upper red and the lower green, at or near the top of the mast

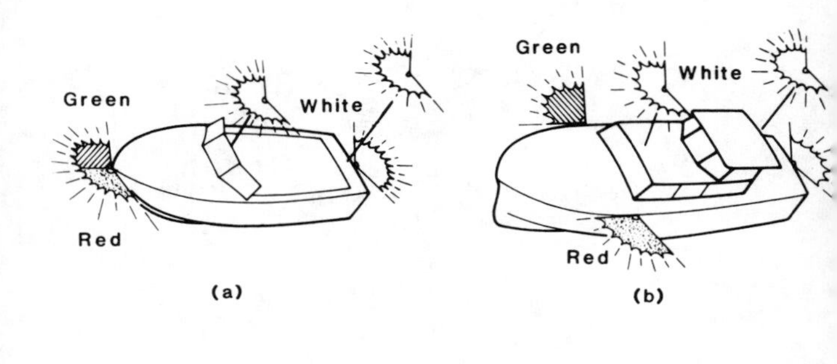

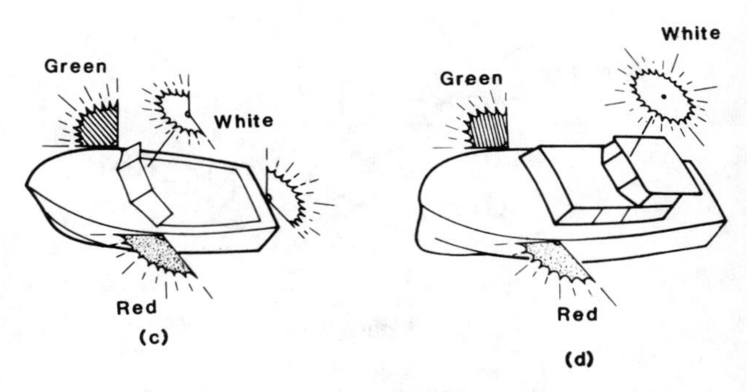

Figure 6-12

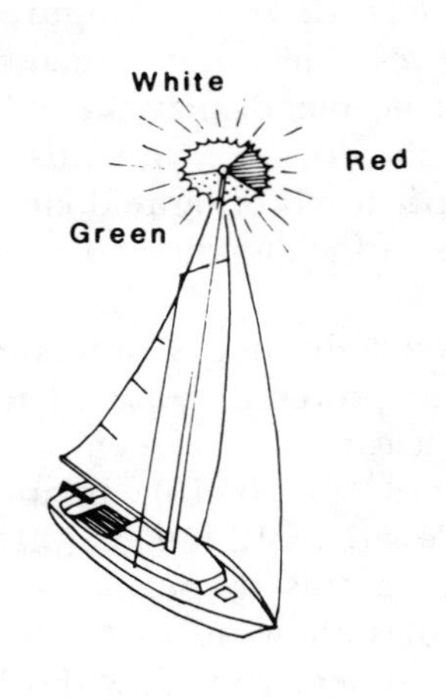

Figure 6-13

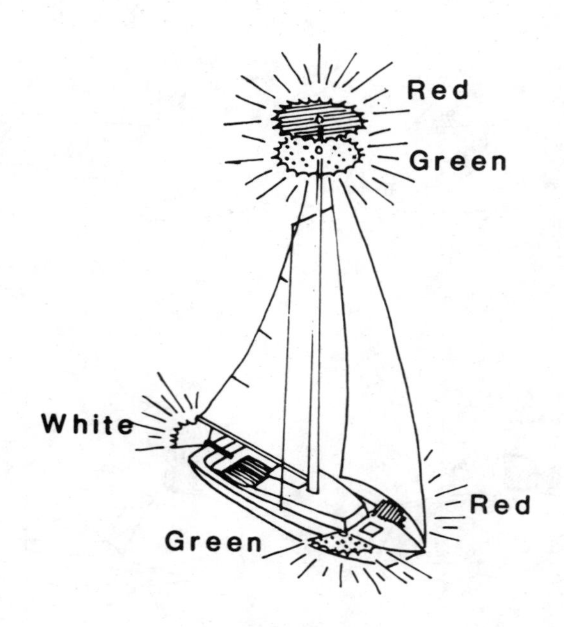

Figure 6-14

where they can best be seen (fig. 6–14). These lights may *not* be exhibited in conjunction with the combined lantern depicted in figure 6–13.

A sailing vessel less than 7 meters (23 ft.) long should, if practicable, display the lights prescribed above. But if she does not, she must have ready at hand an electric torch or lighted lantern to show a white light in sufficient time to prevent collision (fig. 6–15).

During daylight hours, a vessel proceeding under sail and power is required to display forward, where it can best be seen, a conical shape, apex downward (fig. 6–16). Inland Rules state that a vessel less than 12 meters (39 ft. 4 in.) long need not exhibit this shape, but may do so. International Rules allow no such exemption.

A vessel under oars may display the same lights prescribed above for sailing vessels. But if

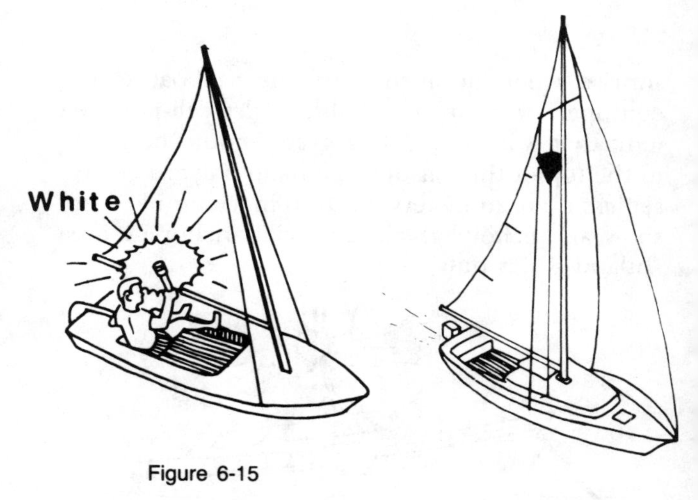

Figure 6-15

Figure 6-16

she does not, she must have ready at hand an electric light or lantern to show a white light in time to prevent collision (fig. 6–17).

A vessel at anchor must display one all-round white light (fig. 6–18) from where it can best be seen. When permanently installed on a sailboat, this light is situated at the top of the mast. The light is displayed between the hours of sunset and

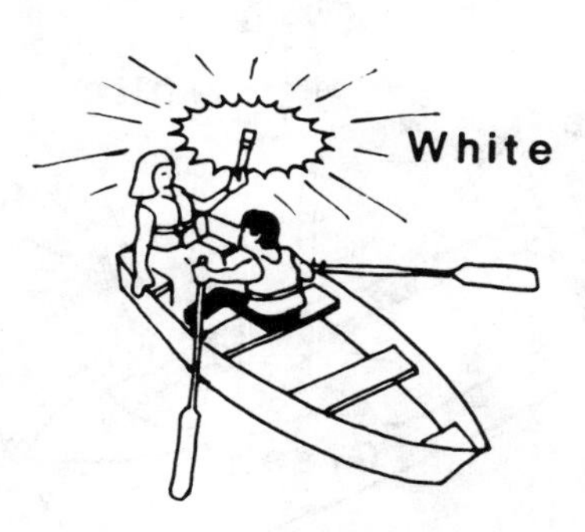

Figure 6-17

sunrise when at anchor. If the sailboat is not equipped with such a light, a dry-cell-powered light that will show 360 degrees should be raised to the top of the mast on the main halyard. A vessel less than 20 meters (65 ft. 6 in.) long need not show an anchor light in a special anchorage area (Inland Rules only).

Figure 6-18

The Rules do not require a vessel of less than 7 meters to show an anchor light when the vessel is not anchored in a navigable area.

A fishing vessel engaged in trawling (dragging a dredge or apparatus used for fishing), when stopped with no way on, must show only

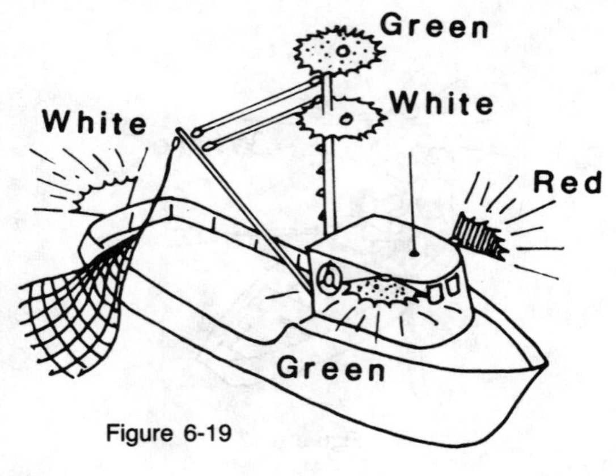

Figure 6-19

two all-round lights in a vertical line, the upper green and the lower white (fig. 6–19).

A fishing vessel engaged in fishing other than trawling, when stopped with no way on, must show only two all-round lights in a vertical line, the upper red and the lower white (fig. 6–20).

When making way through the water, a fishing vessel must also display the customary sidelights and sternlight.

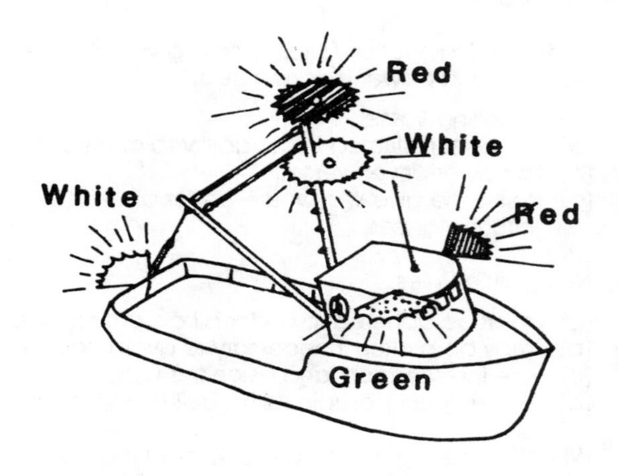

Figure 6-20

Enforcement vessels of federal, state, or local government may display a flashing blue light. This has the same meaning on the water as a flashing blue or red light on police cars on land.

A white strobe light is permitted for a distress signal only.

A good rule to follow: If you see lights other than those you can recognize, keep out of the way.

Section 6: STUDY QUESTIONS FOR NAVIGATION RULES

1. The primary purpose of the Navigation Rules:
   (a) is to prevent collision on the water.
   (b) is to prevent drownings.
   (c) is to make sure you have the necessary equipment on board.
   (d) limits the size of vessel on any given body of water.

2. Under the Navigation Rules, a sailing vessel under both sail and power is considered:
   (a) a sailing vessel.
   (b) a vessel restricted in her ability to maneuver.
   (c) a power-driven vessel.
   (d) to be the give-way vessel under all circumstances.

3. Navigation Rules:
   (a) must be adhered to under all circumstances.
   (b) may be broken if necessary to avoid collision.
   (c) are the same on land as on the water.
   (d) cover every possible risk of collision situation.

4. When two sailing vessels are approaching one another and each has the wind on a different side:
   (a) the vessel which has the wind on the starboard side must keep out of the way of the other.
   (b) both vessels must slow down and determine what the other is doing.
   (c) both vessels must steer to their port side to avoid collision.
   (d) the vessel which has the wind on the port side must keep out of the way of the other.

5. A sailing vessel overtaking a power-driven vessel:

   (a) has the right-of-way.
   (b) must sound three blasts on her whistle.
   (c) is the give-way vessel.
   (d) is the stand-on vessel.

6. When two power-driven vessels are meeting head on or nearly so:

   (a) the vessel with the wind on her port side has the right-of-way.
   (b) the vessel downwind has the right-of-way.
   (c) the vessel to windward has the right-of-way.
   (d) neither vessel has the right-of-way.

7. When two power-driven vessels are crossing so as to involve the risk of collision, the vessel which has the other on her starboard side:

   (a) is the give-way vessel.
   (b) must keep out of the way of the other.
   (c) should alter course, slow down, or stop, in order to avoid collision.
   (d) all of the above.

8. When visibility is restricted, every vessel should:

   (a) post a lookout and proceed with the utmost caution.
   (b) sound proper sound signals and proceed at reduced and safe speed.
   (c) turn on navigation lights.
   (d) all of the above.

9. A vessel's navigation lights:

   (a) are so the skipper can see what lies ahead.
   (b) can be any color as long as they are visible.
   (c) are so the skipper of the other vessel can see her and her heading.
   (d) may only be red and green in color.

10. If you see another vessel's red and white lights off your bow:

    (a) you are in her "danger zone."
    (b) you are the stand-on vessel.
    (c) she is crossing from your port to your starboard.
    (d) none of the above.

11. A sailing vessel, under sail only, and less than 20 meters (65 ft. 7 in.) long:

    (a) must exhibit sidelights and a sternlight visible for 2 miles.
    (b) may combine sidelights and stern light into one fixture carried at or near the top of the mast if in international waters.
    (c) may use a combination lantern at or near the top of the mast when under power.
    (d) all of the above.

12. Sound signals used in passing or crossing situations:

    (a) are to be used at all times.
    (b) are to be used by all vessels whether under sail or power-driven.
    (c) are not to be used under conditions of reduced visibility, unless vessels are in sight of each other.
    (d) are to be given even if the other vessel is not in sight.

13. Two power-driven vessels passing port to port is indicated by:

    (a) two short blasts.
    (b) one short blast.
    (c) three short blasts.
    (d) five or more short blasts.

14. Under the Inland Rules, upon hearing the one or two blast signal, the other vessel, if in agreement, must:

    (a) remain silent.
    (b) sound 4 short blasts.
    (c) sound the same signal.
    (d) answer with a "cross signal."

15. A power-driven vessel intending to overtake another power-driven vessel:

    (a) has the right-of-way.
    (b) must indicate her intention by the proper sound signal.
    (c) should pass the other vessel as close by as possible.
    (d) none of the above.

16. The "danger signal" is:

    (a) rapid and constant waving of arms.
    (b) shouting "danger" as loudly as possible.
    (c) one long blast on the whistle.
    (d) five or more short and rapid blasts on the whistle.

17. Three short blasts on the whistle mean:

    (a) I am coming out of a slip.
    (b) I intend to pass you.
    (c) I am operating astern propulsion.
    (d) danger.

18. When visibility is reduced, a good rule of thumb is to advance only at a speed that allows stopping:

    (a) in the same distance you can see.
    (b) in twice the distance of visibility.
    (c) in half the distance of visibility.
    (d) none of the above.

19. If you are in a powerboat, and only a light wind is blowing, you should pass a sailboat by:

    (a) steering as far away as possible with a minimum wake.
    (b) turning and going behind it so you do not have to slow down.
    (c) staying to windward.
    (d) treating it as you would another powerboat.

20. On a wide, deep lake, under a beautiful blue sky, you are in a powerboat. You approach a group of sailboats, all of which seem to be the same size and going the same direction. Continuing your present course will take you through the middle of this group. You should:

   (a) turn so as to pass on the windward side of all the boats, at least fifty feet away.
   (b) continue course but reduce speed a little because, as the overtaking boat, you have the right-of-way.
   (c) turn so as to pass as far to leeward of the group as possible because they are probably racing.
   (d) slow down and come up alongside one to ask what they are doing.

21. You are running your powerboat in a dredged channel, shown on the chart as 100 feet wide. You realize that you should keep to the right of center. The wind is from dead ahead and the water on each side of the channel is shown to be 4 feet deep. Ahead you see a sailboat crossing the channel from your left. You draw only 2-1/2 feet, so you can turn aside. You decide that you should:

   (a) continue course, but slow down and reduce wake to pass behind the sailboat.
   (b) continue course and speed because she is smaller, slower, and should not be sailing crosswise in the channel.
   (c) speed up to cross ahead of the sailboat.
   (d) slow drastically and try to figure out what she will do next.

A marine radiotelephone is under Federal Communications Commission (FCC) control because it makes use of the public airways. This marine safety device is often misused. On a recreational vessel, the marine radiotelephone has only three legitimate uses: safety communication, operational communication, and ship's business communication. The installation is officially a "shipboard station" and has its individual call letters. For recreational boats the rig must be VHF-FM and of FCC-approved design. Citizens Band (CB) radio has also been authorized by the FCC for marine use but it has limited use as a safety radio.

Radio communication requires a universal call channel over which contact between one station (caller) and another (called) station is made. The latter responds with the number of an available channel on which to talk without blocking safety messages. They both move to that channel, exchange their information, and sign off. A list of VHF-FM Channels and their primary use is found on page 186.

There is a standard format for communicating distress messages which efficiently conveys the nature of the distress and information that will help in relieving it. The form is reproduced here and should be partially filled out for your vessel and posted near the radio.

The shipboard station is required to maintain a radio listening watch on Channel 16 while the radio is on and the vessel is in use, except when it is handling traffic of its own. This is necessary be-

PRIORITY LIST OF VHF–FM CHANNELS FOR RECREATIONAL BOATS

Channel	*Communication Purpose*
06	Intership safety communication (Mandatory).
09	Commercial and noncommercial intership and ship-to-coast (commercial docks, marinas, and some clubs).
12	Port Operations—traffic advisory—still being used as a channel to work USCG shore stations.
13	Navigational—Bridge-to-Bridge (1 watt only) Mandatory for ocean vessels, dredges in channels, and large tugs while towing. This is also the primary channel used at locks and bridges.
14	Port Operations channel for communications with bridge and lock tenders. Some Coast Guard shore stations have this as a working channel.
16	DISTRESS SAFETY and CALLING (Mandatory).
22A	Primary liaison with USCG vessels and USCG shore stations, and for Coast Guard marine information broadcasts.
25	Public telephone (also 24, 27, 84, 85, 86, 87, 88).
26	Public telephone, first priority.
28	Public telephone, first priority.
68	Noncommercial intership and ship-to-coast (marinas, yacht clubs, etc.).
69	Noncommercial intership and ship-to-coast.
71	Noncommercial intership and ship-to-coast.
72	Noncommercial intership, second priority.
78	Noncommercial intership and ship-to-coast.
79	Noncommercial intership and ship-to-coast (Great Lakes only).
80	Noncommercial intership and ship-to-coast (Great Lakes only).
WX-1	Weather broadcasts.
WX-2	Weather broadcasts.
WX-3	Weather broadcasts.

DISTRESS COMMUNICATIONS FORM

Instructions: Complete this form now (except for items 6 through 9) and post near your radiotelephone.

Speak SLOWLY – CLEARLY – CALMLY

1. Make sure your radiotelephone is on.
2. Select either *VHF Channel 16* (156.8 MHz) or *2182* kHz.
3. Press microphone button and say: "MAYDAY – MAYDAY – MAYDAY."
4. Say: "THIS IS ____________ , ____________ , ____________ ."
   your boat name — your boat name — your boat name
5. Say: "MAYDAY ______________________."
   your boat name
6. TELL WHERE YOU ARE (What navigational aids or landmarks are near?).
7. STATE THE NATURE OF YOUR DISTRESS.
8. GIVE NUMBER OF ADULTS AND CHILDREN ABOARD, AND CONDITIONS OF ANY INJURED.
9. ESTIMATE PRESENT SEAWORTHINESS OF YOUR BOAT.
10. BRIEFLY DESCRIBE YOUR BOAT:

    ______________________________ (Type) ______________________________ (Length) FEET

    ____________ (Draft) FEET; ____________ (Color) HULL; ____________ (Color) TRIM;

    ____________ (Number) MASTS; ____________ (Type; Horsepower) POWER: ____________ (Construction Material) .

    ____
    Anything else you think will help rescuers to find you
11. Say "I WILL BE LISTENING ON *CHANNEL 16 / 2182*."
    (Cross out channel no. or frequency that does not apply)
12. End Message by saying: "THIS IS ________________ OVER,"
    your boat name
13. Release microphone button and listen: Someone should answer. IF THEY DO NOT, REPEAT CALL, BEGINNING AT ITEM 3. If there is still no answer, switch to another channel and begin again.

VESSEL INFORMATION DATA SHEET

When requesting assistance from the Coast Guard, you may be asked to furnish the following details. This list should, therefore, be filled out as completely as possible and posted alongside your transmitter with the *Distress Communications Form.*

1. **Description of Vessel Requiring Assistance.**

Sail;______, Power: Inboard______, Outboard______, I/O______

Type of vessel: (Ketch, sloop, sedan or express cruiser, row boat, etc.)

________________. Manufacturer or class________________

Boat Length________. Draft________. Home Port______________

Hull Markings (color trim, etc.)______________________________

2. **Survival Gear Aboard**

Personal Flotation Devices ____
Flares ____
Flashlight ____
Raft ____
Dinghy or Tender ____
Anchor ____
Spotlight ____
Auxilliary power ____
Horn ____

3. **Electronic Equipment**

Radiotelephone(s) VHF MF HF
Channels/Frequencies available
VHF Channel 22A ____
MF–2670 kHz ____
Radar ____
Depth Finder ____
Loran ____
Direction Finder ____
EPIRB ____

4. **Vessel Owner/Operator**

Name____

Telephone Number__________________________________

Address____

Is Owner/Operator an experienced sailor? Yes No

5. **Miscellaneous**

Be prepared to describe the local weather conditions, depth of water etc.

cause any vessel may be able to provide help in the case of an emergency.

CALLING PROCEDURE

The official format for making a call goes like this: You are the radio operator aboard the *Queen* and set out to call your friend's boat the *Annie*:

Queen: "Annie! Annie! Annie! This is *Queen*—".

If he does not respond, wait two minutes (mandatory) and call again. Now he answers:

Annie: "Queen, this is *Annie*—switch to 68."

Queen: "Roger 68."

Both vessels switch to Channel 68.

Queen: "Annie! This is *Queen*."

Annie: "This is *Annie*."

With their conversation initiated they have three minutes to talk. When the conversation ends, each announces his boat name and leaves the air. Do not add unnecessary words or phrases.

There are three kinds of radio emergency communications and each has its own call sign:

MAYDAY, MAYDAY, MAYDAY is restricted to a situation in which a life or vessel is in immediate danger.

PAN-PAN, PAN-PAN, PAN-PAN is an urgency signal indicating a person or vessel is in jeopardy to a degree less than MAYDAY.

SECURITY, SECURITY, SECURITY introduces a message about a matter of navigational safety or weather warning.

Section 6: STUDY QUESTIONS FOR MARINE RADIOTELEPHONE

1. The primary type of radiotelephone used in boating for short-range communication is:

   (a) VHF–AM
   (b) Citizens Band (CB)
   (c) Single Side Band (SSB)
   (d) VHF–FM

2. Radio calls are typically initiated on Channel:

   (a) 6
   (b) 9
   (c) 16
   (d) 22A

3. You purchase a VHF–FM marine radio telephone. The license(s) required are:

   (a) a station license for the radio.
   (b) an operator's license for yourself.
   (c) both of the above.
   (d) no licenses needed for VHF–FM.

4. You have an emergency situation and make a "MAYDAY" call. This call is initiated on Channel:

   (a) 6
   (b) 16
   (c) 22
   (d) 70

5. The marine radiotelephone can legally be used for the purpose of:

   (a) arranging a rendezvous.
   (b) determining where fuel is available.
   (c) the ship's safety, operation, and business.
   (d) all the above.

6. You wish to contact a marina. The conversation will most likely be done on Channel:
   (a) 6
   (b) 9
   (c) 13
   (d) 16

7. Citizens Band radios:
   (a) are not authorized for marine use.
   (b) are monitored by the Coast Guard.
   (c) require special licenses for marine application.
   (d) have limited use as a safety radio.

8. The Distress Communications Form:
   (a) is required on all boats over 26 feet.
   (b) is an aid for making organized distress calls.
   (c) must be completed prior to making a distress call.
   (d) all the above.

Successful trailering requires a proper trailer, a towing vehicle with the weight and power to pull the rig, and the proper hitch.

THE TRAILER

Legal Requirements

Trailer towing laws vary between states, so be sure to determine the legal trailer and towing requirements in each state in which you will tow your boat. Automobile associations, boating clubs, or law enforcement agencies are logical places to get this information.

Classification. Trailers are divided into classes based on the total weight of the trailer and its load. However, if the total weight runs more than 85 percent of the maximum weight for a class, you should select a trailer of the next higher class.

CLASS	MAXIMUM GROSS WEIGHT
I	2,000 lbs (907.2 kg)
II	3,500 lbs (1,587.6 kg)
III	5,000 lbs (2,268.0 kg)
IV	Over 5,000 lbs

Federal law requires that all trailers have capacity information displayed on a plate similar to the one in figure 6–21.

On multiaxle trailers, the combined Gross Axle Weight Rating (GAWR) of all axles must be equal to or greater than the Gross Vehicle Weight

Rating (GVWR) for the trailer. This capacity information will show the size of tires needed to carry the load for which the trailer is rated.

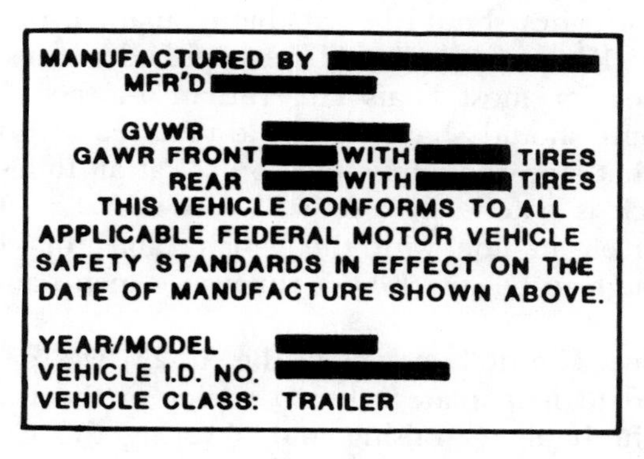

MANUFACTURED BY
MFR'D

GVWR
GAWR FRONT WITH TIRES
REAR WITH TIRES
THIS VEHICLE CONFORMS TO ALL APPLICABLE FEDERAL MOTOR VEHICLE SAFETY STANDARDS IN EFFECT ON THE DATE OF MANUFACTURE SHOWN ABOVE.

YEAR/MODEL
VEHICLE I.D. NO.
VEHICLE CLASS: TRAILER

Figure 6-21

Trailer Features

Coupler. The coupler attaches the trailer to the hitch. It is generally a latch or screw type (fig. 6–22).

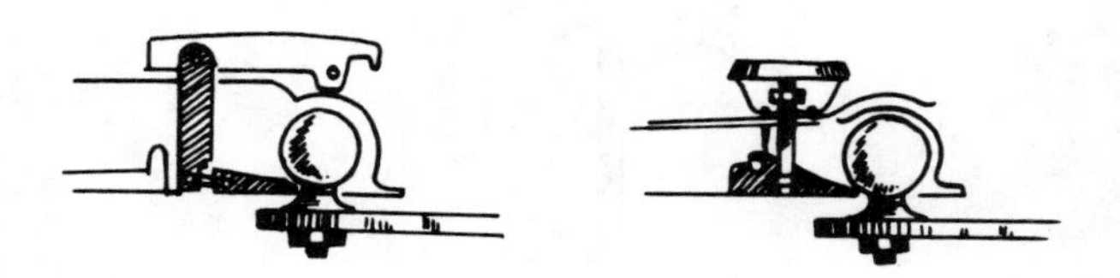

Figure 6-22

The coupler must match the ball. The size of the ball is determined by the Gross Vehicle Weight Rating (GVWR). All couplers manufactured after 1973 will have the Gross Vehicle Weight Rating stamped on them.

Winch. Electric and manual winches are available. Both types should be equipped with brakes. Electric winches should be capable of manual operation. Fiber ropes should be replaced with steel cables for most boats larger than 14 feet. The winch should have an anti-reverse, two-way ratchet stop for safety and control at all times. A winch is potentially a lethal weapon. *Never* place yourself in line with the winch cable, or close enough to be struck by a runaway winch handle.

Dolly. The dolly assembly (fig. 6–23) was developed to help mate a heavy trailer to the trailer hitch. It allows raising and lowering the trailer tongue and facilitates moving the trailer for parking and other purposes. Raising the trailer tongue will also tilt the boat to allow for drainage.

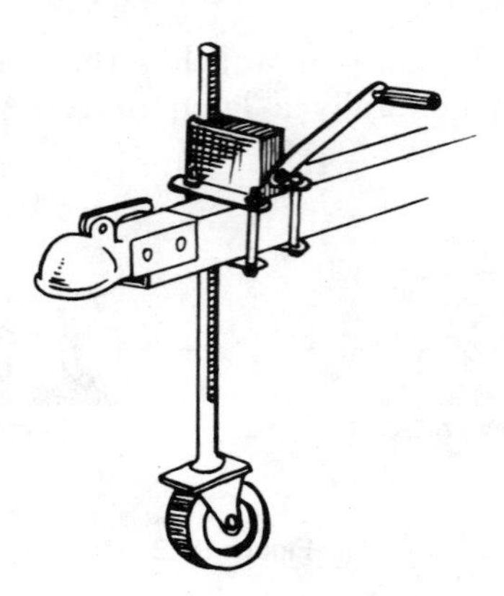

Figure 6-23

Supports. While in the water, the boat hull is supported by even pressure over the entire bottom surface. The best boat trailer cannot duplicate the support found in the water. But so much of the boat's life is spent on the trailer that it should be given the best possible support. Improper supports have caused split bottoms and other hull damage, so skimping on the trailer is false economy. Boat trailers have two types of supports:

Rollers provide minimum support but are more efficient for loading and launching because of minimum friction (fig. 6–24). They must be carefully positioned to provide even support for the hull.

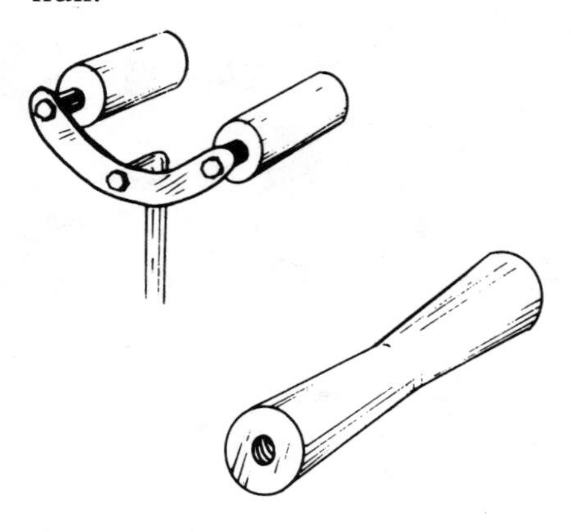

Figure 6-24

Padded Bolsters provide maximum support, but are more troublesome for loading and launching because of excessive friction (fig. 6–25).

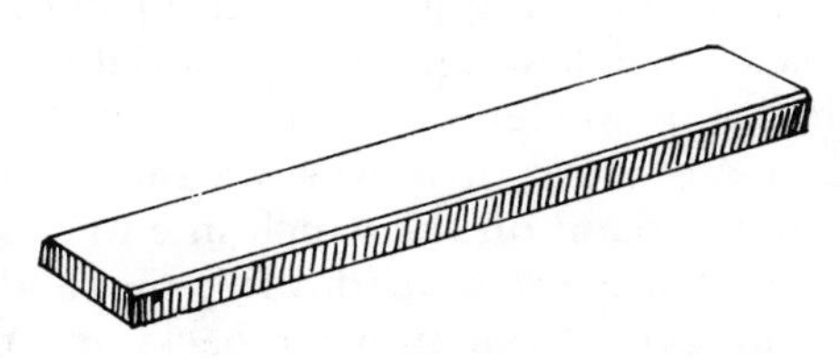

Figure 6-25

There are four vital support points for most hulls: (1) under the bow, (2) the keel, (3) at the turn of the bilge especially where interior weights are concentrated, and (4) the transom, shown in figure 6–26.

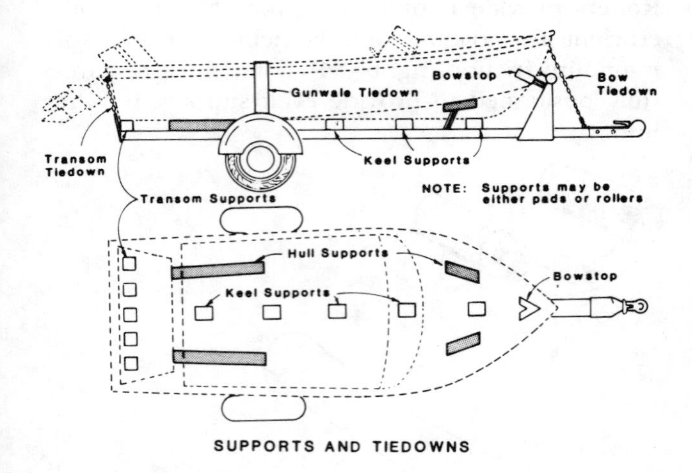

Figure 6-26

Rollers and pads can be adjusted up and down as well as forward and backward, to provide the best possible support. When any part that has a matching component on the other side of the trailer is adjusted, it is important to ensure that both are adjusted properly to oppose each other.

Tie-downs. To prevent the boat from sliding off the trailer or becoming misaligned during travel, tie-downs are needed (fig. 6–27). Special hooks or loops should be welded to the trailer for that purpose. Bow and stern tie-downs are the most crucial. Do not depend on the winch line to hold the bow in place; use a bow tie-down. Bow tie-downs prevent the boat from moving backward if the winch line breaks, and prevent the boat from

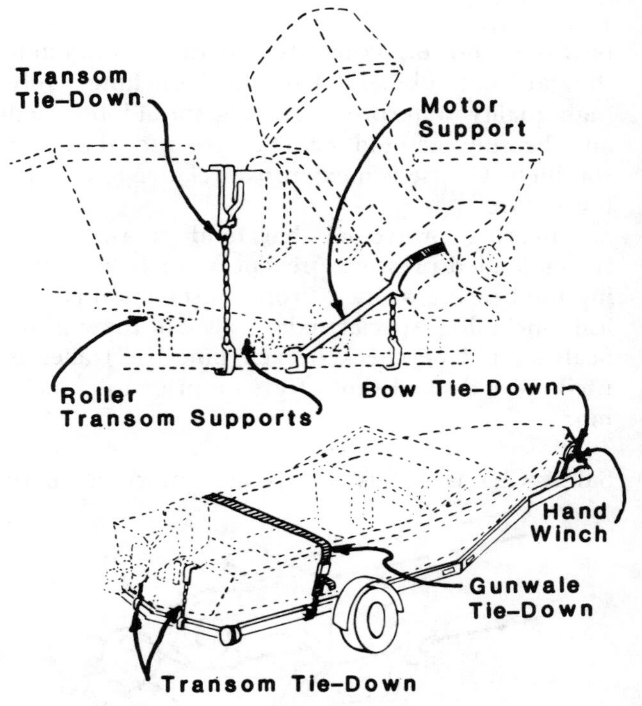

Figure 6-27

going over the top of the bow stop in the event of a sudden stop or accident.

Tires. The size and weight-carrying capacity of tires vary greatly. Federal law requires that the load capacity and other important information be legibly displayed on the sidewall of the tire. To eliminate the need for two spare tires, it may be possible to order a trailer with the same size wheels, tires, and bolt pattern as those on the towing vehicle. The load-carrying ability of a tire varies with inflation, so it is important to check tire pressure routinely.

Bearings and Bearing Protectors. Trailer wheel

bearings require special care and attention, even if they are not submerged during launching. Only high-quality waterproof greases should be used and bearings should be checked and repacked routinely. Grease is inexpensive relative to a bearing failure.

Bearing protectors that hold grease under spring-loaded pressure prevent water from entering the bearing proper. Proper installation is critical, including special axle seals on the inside. Seals should be checked each time the trailer is used. Give a small shot of grease prior to launching.

Safety Chains. Safety chains, an important safety

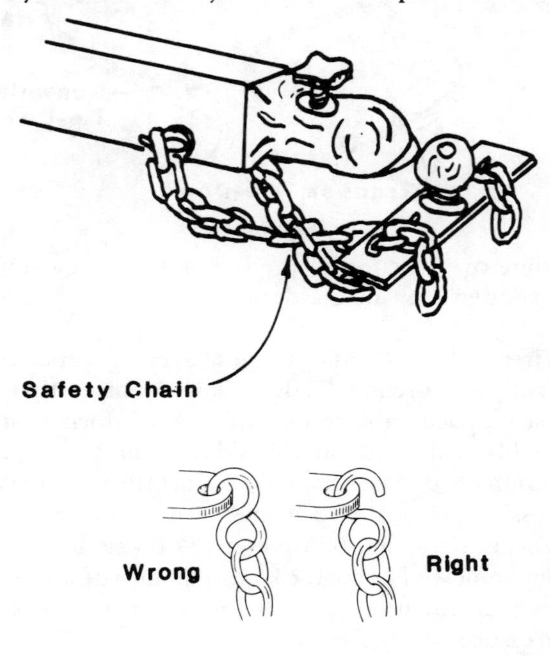

Figure 6-28

feature, are legally required. They should be permanently affixed to the trailer and crossed under the hitch in such a way that they will catch and hold the tongue should the ball fail. The chains should be attached to the towing vehicle at points separate from the ball and the bracket that holds the ball. Most trailers are factory supplied with "S" hooks on their safety chains. A more positive method is to replace the "S" hooks with heavy duty shackles and screw pins. Some states require a shackle or clevis in place of "S" hooks.

Trailer Brakes. Although laws differ, most states require brakes on trailers above a certain gross weight, and some specify the types that are acceptable. The three most popular braking systems in use today are: surge brakes, electric brakes, and electrically actuated hydraulic brakes. You should select trailer brakes that are actuated by the brakes of the towing vehicle. An emergency breakaway system, required in some states, is a recommended feature.

Trailer Lights. Every trailer must have lights, including tail, brake, license plate lights, and turn signals. Also sidelights and reflectors may be required. The tow vehicle must have a heavy-duty flasher relay in the turn-signal circuit and a trailer light harness, available from your dealer or auto parts supplier. Stranded wire is recommended to reduce vibration damage. Note there must be a separate ground from the car to the trailer, usually part of the wiring harness.

Trailer Finish. A good anti-rust treatment covered by a high-quality enamel or spray paint or hot-dip galvanizing will help prevent corrosion. Give the trailer a good wash after each use.

THE TOW VEHICLE

You should not tow a trailer heavier than your car. Check with your dealer for the manufacturer's recommendations on the best towing package. Packages include such items as a nonslip differential, heavy-duty cooling system, heavy-duty flasher, oversize battery and alternator, heavy-duty suspension, special wiring, special rear-axle ratio, and larger tires and wheels.

Tow Vehicle Features

Adequate Power. The two vehicle must have enough power to merge safely with highway traffic when towing maximum load. It must also be able to climb commonly encountered hills without losing speed.

Cooling. For cooling, the engine may need a heavy-duty, high-capacity radiator with extra core tubes to speed heat release, possibly a special fan shroud, a coolant recovery unit, and a thermostat-operated spray-coolant unit to spray cool water on the radiator core tubes when the temperature of the coolant goes too high.

Transmission. Towing a trailer places an extra load on the transmission. This may generate enough heat to burn the transmission fluid and damage the transmission. An external cooler can be installed in series with the radiator coil to provide additional cooling of the transmission fluid. The driver of a towing vehicle must always be on the alert for transmission fluid leaks, slippage, or rough shifting, all of which indicate transmission problems.

Brakes. Cars ordered with a towing option have

oversized drums and/or special heavy-duty brake linings. Standard auto brakes are under size for towing all but very light trailers. Brakes should have premium linings, especially on the rear wheels.

Suspension System. One hundred pounds of tongue weight 4 feet behind the rear axle has the same effect as 400 pounds added to the trunk of the car. To avoid excessive sagging and "bottoming out," the suspension should be reinforced with heavy-duty springs, air shocks, or air bags. Heavy-duty shock absorbers are necessary to control the added weight. These modifications allow the vehicle to ride in a near-normal attitude and improve visibility and handling.

Choosing a Hitch

The rear of a tow vehicle is generally loaded with luggage, gear, and family members. When the tongue weight of a loaded trailer is added, a heavy strain is placed on the rear tires. It is important, therefore, to properly choose the class of hitch for the weight of the trailer being towed. There are two basic types of hitches: the weight-carrying hitch and the weight-distribution (or load-equalizer) hitch.

Hitch Classes. The class of hitch required will depend on the gross trailer weight and its tongue weight (fig. 6–29). The dealer who supplies the towing vehicle can normally provide guidance.

Weight-carrying Hitch. The simplest and most inexpensive hitch is the so-called bumper hitch, mounted on the rear bumper of the car. It may be adequate for light trailers, but it is not recommended and is banned in several states. The "step-bumper" hitch mounted on many light trucks is not considered a bumper hitch. Weight-carrying hitches come in various sizes and configurations depending on gross trailer weight, tongue weight, and tow-vehicle characteristics. As the name implies, the weight-carrying hitch supports the entire weight of the trailer tongue (fig. 6–29[a] and [b]).

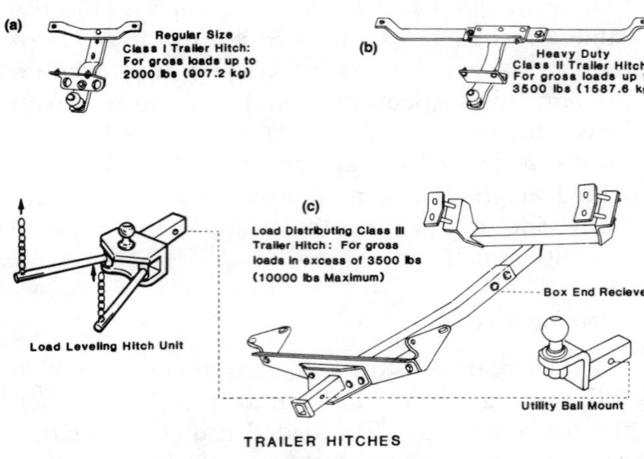

TRAILER HITCHES

Figure 6-29

Weight-distribution Hitch. A heavy trailer may place so much weight on the rear of the car resulting in too much weight being removed from the front wheels. Control becomes difficult and operation dangerous. A "weight-distribution" or "load equalizer" hitch redistributes much of this weight to all four wheels of the tow vehicle as well as the wheels of the trailer, resulting in better handling, safer operation, and less wear and tear on the tow vehicle. Figure 6–29(c) shows the two components of a weight-distributing hitch: (1) the box frame receiver unit that is welded or bolted to the vehicle frame, and (2) the hitch unit with load leveling beams and tension adjusting chains. If the frame unit is used with a utility ball mount, the unit is simply a heavy duty weight-carrying hitch.

Some weight-distribution hitches are equipped with "anti-sway bars," which help control trailer sway and improve control.

Extra care must be exercised when a trailer is equipped with surge activated, hydraulic brakes. When the equalizer beam tension adjusting chains are "snubbed up" too tightly, they can interfere with the brake actuation mechanism, and thus prevent the brakes from operating properly, if at all. Some trailer manufacturers warn that their brake warranty will be voided if a load equalizing hitch is used. Electrically actuated brakes are not affected.

Ball. The ball that connects the towing vehicle with the trailer is a critical part of the hitch and must be of the proper size. It must be bolted with a lock washer to the proper tongue, or welded when required.

RECOMMENDED BALL DIAMETERS

Class	Max. Weight	Ball Diameter
I	2,000 lbs	1 7/8 inches (47.6 mm)
II	3,500 lbs	2 inches (50.8 mm)
III	10,000 lbs	2 5/16 inches (57.9 mm)

Tongue Weight. The weight on the trailer coupler ball (tongue weight) is determined by (1) the position of the boat on the trailer and (2) the longitudinal placement of the axle on the trailer frame. Either or both of these may be adjusted to attain the optimum tongue weight on the ball—between 5 and 10 percent of the Gross Vehicle Weight (GVW). Remember that the GVW includes all normal gear stowed aboard. A good guideline is that a trailer with sufficient tongue weight will not "fishtail" when being towed at cruising speed whereas one with too little tongue weight will.

Determining the tongue weight is not difficult. First, with the loaded hitch on a level surface, place a bathroom scale below the trailer coupler. On this, place a sturdy box that will support the tongue at the exact towing height previously determined. Now remove the trailer coupler from the tow vehicle ball and place it on the box. The tongue and trailer frame should now be parallel to the paved surface beneath it. If so, read the tongue weight on the scale. The tongue weight for passenger cars without special suspensions should not be more than 100 pounds nor be less than 40 pounds. If the weight is more than 75 pounds, use a dolly or tongue jack to avoid injury when positioning the trailer. Bear in mind that 50 gallons of fuel and water weigh about 375 pounds and could drastically affect the final results.

If you have a dual-axle trailer, the results of the following experiment may surprise you. On a level surface, place the tongue jack on the scale and disengage the hitch. Observe the reading as you raise the tongue or lower it. The tongue weight changes as you shift the center of gravity from the front to the rear. This explains the necessity for a level trailer frame when determining the tongue weight.

TRAILER OPERATION

Trailering a boat presents only a few problems when moving forward on a dry pavement at moderate speeds during the day. When operating the rig for the first time, choose ideal conditions and a lightly traveled road. In turning corners, swing a little wider than you would with the car alone, but signal your turn, and watch for cars in the outside lane. The distance between your car and the one ahead should be increased by at least two car lengths, or doubled at higher speeds. On a clear stretch, practice gentle braking to get the feel. Note any tendency of the trailer to sway or jackknife.

After driving a mile or so, pull well off the highway and check everything, including the temperature of the wheel bearings by feeling the hubs. Check tie-downs, cover, wheel lug-nuts, and other fastenings every hour or two.

The added load will make a difference in the braking and acceleration of the tow vehicle. More room will be needed to stop. Greater clear distance will be necessary for overtaking and passing other vehicles; don't try it until you feel comfortable with the rig. Don't be impatient!

Maneuvering the Trailer

There is a knack to maneuvering a vehicle and trailer in close quarters, especially when backing up. That is best learned by practice. Begin with an empty trailer in an empty parking lot or school yard. (Sunday may be a good day.) Use empty boxes, plastic bottles, or lined parking spaces as target areas to back into. The first lesson is to learn how to back in a straight line and then how to turn while backing to put the trailer where you want it.

When you have the car and trailer aligned, put the car in reverse. Take your time—the key to success is proceeding slowly.

Put your hand on the bottom of the steering wheel. *A trailer always backs in a direction opposite to that of the tow vehicle.* The trick is to move the bottom of the steering wheel in the same direction as you want the trailer to go. By turning the wheel to the right, the front of the car will go to the left; but the trailer will turn right.

Start moving slowly in reverse. With the trailer and vehicle initially aligned, the trailer will move straight back if the wheel is held straight;

but only for a short distance. When the trailer starts to move to the right or left, you must move the bottom of the steering wheel in the direction opposite the direction the trailer is moving. Try to correct a small misalignment with a small movement of the wheel.

When you wish to turn when backing, move the bottom of the steering wheel in the direction you wish to go.

As the trailer starts to turn, bring the wheel back to the straight position. The trailer will continue to turn, but at an increasing rate. You must move the bottom of the wheel opposite to the direction the trailer is moving in order to stop the increasing rate of turn of the rig. When backing a rig, you will find that frequent small corrections will be required whether you are turning or going straight.

If the trailer does not turn sharply enough, or turns so far as to "jackknife," just stop, pull ahead a few feet to straighten out, and try again.

Figure 6–30 depicts backing a trailer into a ramp. In (a), the car and trailer are aligned, but at an angle to the ramp. The initial move will be straight back. In (b), the driver turns the wheel left so the trailer moves left into the ramp. In (c), the driver reverses the car wheels to stop the trailer from turning and to get the car and trailer realigned. At (d), the driver straightens the car wheels when the car and trailer are aligned with the ramp and continues backing the trailer to the water. When there is room, of course, you may make a wide swing going ahead, then come to a stop where the trailer may be backed straight back with no turns required, but this will rarely be possible at most ramps.

Practice and more practice is the only way to acquire skill in maneuvering a car and trailer at the beach or a busy ramp. By all means, get in a

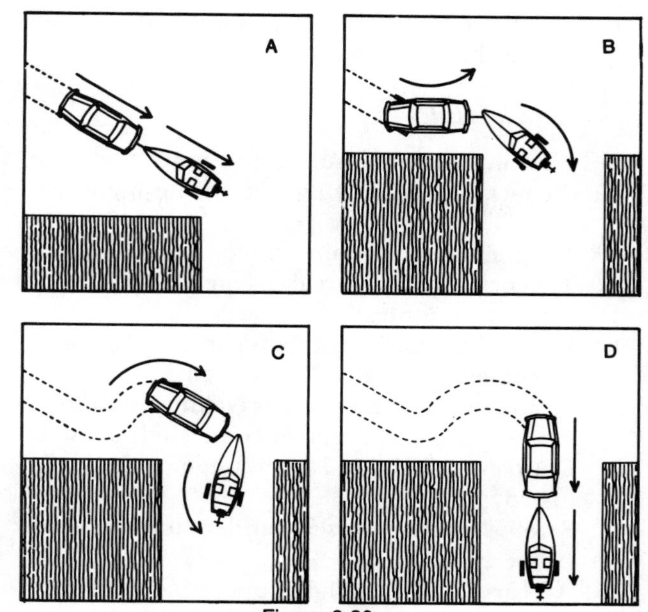

Figure 6-30

lot of daytime practice before trying your first nighttime driving.

Pre-Trip Checklist

So that you have time to make adjustments or repairs before hooking up, make sure in advance that:

1. Trailer wheel bearings are greased.
2. Trailer tires are at correct pressure.
3. Spare tires, jacks, and parts are in usable condition.
4. Boat's steering mechanism is working smoothly. If frozen from lack of lubrication, lubricate it and free up its movement.
5. All boat connections and linkages are tight. Trailering subjects the boat to abnormal jolting and vibration, so connections and linkages

do come loose. This can be disastrous on the water at high speed.

Pre-Road Checklist

Following is a minimum list of items that you should check before starting out on the highway:

1. Tongue weight within limits.
2. Tilt lock secured (break-frame trailers).
3. Tie-downs secured.
4. Winch line taut. Anti-reverse gear latched. Turnbuckle or safety hook secure.
5. Motor in recommended traveling position.
6. Home battery charger disconnected, if used.
7. Coupler ball tight. Lower finger clamp adjusted.
8. Safety chains crossed under tongue and properly fastened.
9. All car and trailer lights operating properly.
10. Trailer and car brakes operable.
11. Car rearview mirrors in proper position.
12. Boat folding top down and secured. It can flip a trailer.
13. All loose gear in boat secured.
14. Boat cover secured.
15. If a sailboat, mast and rigging secured and red flags on projections over stern.
16. All ensigns, burgees, or flags removed and secured.
17. If everything checks, walk around the rig again, just to make sure.

On the Road

Always start slowly, in low gear, and take the car up through the gears gently. Once under way, never forget that you have a boat behind you. This sounds foolish, but when you're traveling along at highway speeds, it is all too easy to lose a feel for the tow—until you have to pass, turn, or brake. Think twice about passing other vehicles—but if you decide to pass, don't delay. Be alert for signs restricting trailers.

Remain sensitive to unusual sounds or handling factors, and if there's anything that seems unusual, pull over immediately and check. In fact, you should pull over and check the entire rig every hour or so. Check for high temperatures in the wheel bearings, wheel lug-nuts, loosened tie-downs, lights, tire pressure, and car engine temperature.

On-the-road things to remember:

1. Never let anyone ride in the trailer. It is dangerous, and illegal in many states.
2. Observe speed limits. In many states, the speed limit for cars towing a trailer is lower than for a car traveling by itself.
3. Maintain a greater following distance between your vehicle and the one in front of you. With the trailer, you need much more room to stop.
4. When traveling over bumpy roads or crossing railroad tracks, slow down. Going too fast may cause the tow vehicle to bottom out and the hitch to scrape, damaging both car and trailer.
5. Large trucks and buses create considerable turbulence, which may cause the trailer to fishtail. Keep a firm grip on the steering wheel and tension on the hitch ball. If there is a manual lever that operates the trailer brakes separately from those on the car, a quick application of the trailer brakes may slow the trailer sufficiently to eliminate sway.

At the Launch Site

Usually the trailer boater has completed a trip of an hour or more. High-speed towing causes wheel bearings to get hot. When the hot bearings are immersed in cold water, the almost instant contraction of the air in the bearing draws water in through the grease seals. Even so-called waterproof seals may not prevent this. It is best to wait until the bearings have cooled before launching.

A trailer boater may install a hitch on the front bumper of the tow vehicle to simplify maneuvers at the ramp. He backs the trailer to the ramp, unhitches on level ground (chocking the wheels), turns the tow vehicle around, and hooks up to the front hitch. He can then drive the tow vehicle forward to move the trailer into the water. This also keeps the rear wheels of the tow vehicle on dry land when launching at unpaved ramps.

A considerate boater does not occupy the ramp any longer than necessary for safe launching. You should make most of your preparations before moving to the ramp.

1. With a break-frame trailer, leave the tilt mechanism and anti-reverse gear locked. They must not be released until you are actually ready to launch.
2. Check to see that the boat drain plugs are in tight.
3. Have chocks for the car wheels handy.
4. With a large powerboat, lower the cradles or secondary supports.
5. With a deep-draft sailboat, leave in the main supports so it won't topple over.
6. If possible, step the mast of a sailboat here. Check for power lines first.
7. Load all necessary equipment.
8. Make bow and stern lines fast to proper boat cleats.
9. If boat is to go alongside a pier, rig fenders on the proper side.
10. Remove boat tie-downs.

11. Make sure to double-check the drain plugs.
12. Inspect ramp conditions, water depth, drop-off, obstructions, wind, and current. With a sailboat, check again for overhead power lines, which could kill if the mast struck them. Don't guess that they'll miss!

Launching

1. Back straight down the ramp, having your mate or crewman direct you. If possible, stop with the trailer wheels at the water's edge, unsubmerged. Do not wet the wheel bearings until they have cooled.
2. Chock the wheels of the tow vehicle so that the trailer does not pull it into the water.
3. Have your mate or crewman hold free ends of bow and stern lines, from the ramp.
4. With a break-frame trailer, adjust mechanism and release lock.
5. Release winch ratchet and allow boat to slide off the trailer. Keep your body and face away from the winch handle! Wear heavy gloves when handling the winch cable.
6. Secure the trailer tilt lock; remove winch cable from the bow.
7. Beach the bow of the boat, or pull to pier or float, and secure it.
8. If launching a sailboat, lower the centerboard and attach rudder as soon as water is deep enough.
9. Clear the ramp area; park the car and trailer. If possible, wash off salt water.
10. Lock motor or I/O foot in the down position. Connect fuel lines from portable tanks. Check to be sure that fuel lines are unrestricted, and that there are no gas fumes. Start engine and let warm up.
11. Depart launching area slowly. If wind is blowing onto the pier move with the stern

into the wind. Take in fenders; coil and stow lines.

Hauling Out

Again, courtesy demands that all necessary preparations be made aboard the boat before moving to the ramp.

1. Secure fuel lines from portable tanks. Lock outboard motor or I/O in the up position.
2. Sailboat: raise centerboard and raise or remove rudder.
3. If it is windy, a stern line may be needed to help guide the boat to and onto the trailer; the person holding it should be well to the windward side of the ramp.
4. Back the trailer down the ramp, submerging it only as far as a previously marked line.
5. Guide the boat onto the trailer; hook up the winch line.
6. As the boat is cranked onto the trailer, keep your hands and arms clear. If the boat is not properly aligned on the supports, refloat it and try again.
7. While the boat is tilted, open the drain plugs.
8. Rig a couple of tie-downs and promptly clear the ramp if others are waiting. Pick up your wheel chocks.
9. If in salt water, wash down trailer and boat hull with fresh water as soon as possible.
10. Sailboat: unstep and secure mast and rigging. Check for power lines.
11. Secure everything for the road; after a walk-around check, haul away.

Sailboat Trailering

Many sailboats can be carried on trailers and launched in the same manner as powerboats. In fact, some are specially designed for trailering and are sold with a matching trailer.

While some sailboats can be rolled off the trailer into the water, it is common for many sailboats to be supported by padded bolsters or bars, thereby requiring a launch ramp deep enough to float the boat off the trailer or have the boat lifted off the trailer with a crane. The padded bunks or rollers must be adjusted to provide adequate support for the keel, or any area of the hull where there is a heavy concentration of weight—such as an auxiliary engine.

Sailboats are trailered with the masts unstepped and carried in a horizontal position. Special holders for the spars may be on the boat itself, or on the trailer.

EXTRA CARE MUST BE TAKEN WHEN LAUNCHING OR RETRIEVING, AND WHEN STEPPING OR UNSTEPPING THE MAST, TO BE SURE THERE ARE NO OVERHEAD, HIGH-VOLTAGE, ELECTRICAL WIRES IN THE VICINITY THAT COULD COME IN CONTACT WITH THE MAST OR RIGGING.

Severe electrical shock or electrocution is imminent.

When the sailboat is pulled out of the water on her trailer, she must be unrigged and, as with a powerboat, carefully secured for highway travel.

Post-Trip Checklist

After running in salt water, remove loose items from cockpit, close cuddy cabin, and hose down with fresh water, inside and out, including motor and trailer. This will extend the life of everything.

Examine the propeller(s) for nicks or damage, or fishing lines. Wipe down all hardware with a clean, soft rag. Spray with an aerosol demoisturant, including snaps on curtains.

Keep the wheel bearings of the trailer free of water. Water can run into the hubs and emulsify the grease. Examine and repack as necessary, at least twice a year. Do not allow hubs to freeze while containing water, or seals may rupture. Keep electrical connections or sockets dry. Keep hitch greased, and winch lubricated.

Storage. To prevent water from accumulating in the boat, remove the drain plug and tilt the trailer enough to allow drainage. This should be done for even short-term storage.

When storing the boat on its trailer for any length of time, you can make tires last longer by getting weight off the wheels. Cinder blocks under the tongue and four corners of the trailer frame, shimmed up if necessary by boards, should be adequate support. Once the trailer is jacked up, check to be sure that the boat is evenly supported—the trailer frame can easily be bent out of shape by excessive jacking at one corner.

Covers. Your boat cover should be tailored to your specific boat to stay in place under a variety of conditions. A top drawstring allows for pulling the cover high enough to shed water. Remember that water puddles in the cover must be prevented since water weighs about 8.3 pounds per gallon. The weight of collected water stretches the cover and the water is allowed to funnel into the boat. A bottom drawstring and tie-downs, which go under the boat, are handy to prevent the cover from whipping in the wind. Sandbags or other weights sewn into pockets along the bottom drawstring will help keep the cover in place.

Covering tires during storage extends their life by protecting them from harmful rays of the sun.

Section 6: STUDY QUESTIONS FOR BOAT TRAILERING

1. Trailers are classified according to:

   (a) length.
   (b) width.
   (c) weight.
   (d) all of the above.

2. You should have the next larger trailer if your trailer load is more than———percent of maximum capacity.

   (a) 15
   (b) 85
   (c) 25
   (d) 40

3. The winch line on a boat trailer for a boat 20 feet long should be made of:

   (a) nylon.
   (b) polypropylene.
   (c) steel cable.
   (d) any of the above.

4. Supports are vital under:

   (a) the keel.
   (b) the transom.
   (c) where interior weights are concentrated.
   (d) all of the above.

5. Trailer tire pressure should conform to manufacturer's specification. Tire pressure should be checked:

   (a) after a long trip on the highway.
   (b) when the trailer is not loaded.
   (c) before starting when the tires are cold.
   (d) once a year.

6. Safety chains from the trailer to the hitch are:

   (a) crossed chains under the tongue.
   (b) a good idea but optional.
   (c) basically unnecessary.
   (d) essential only for insurance purposes.

7. Brake lights and turn signals are required on:

   (a) all trailers.
   (b) only when using a trailer at night.
   (c) only on trailers under 5,000 pounds.
   (d) only on trailers over 5,000 pounds.

8. If you pull a trailer with your passenger car, you may need to increase the capability of the:

   (a) suspension system.
   (b) lights.
   (c) cooling system.
   (d) both a and c.

9. Use of a bumper hitch is:

   (a) not recommended.
   (b) acceptable for all sizes of boats.
   (c) legal in all states.
   (d) none of the above.

10. The proper class of trailer hitch for your rig is based on:

    (a) trailer length.
    (b) tow vehicle weight.
    (c) gross trailer weight.
    (d) all of the above.

11. A weight distribution hitch transfers much of the weight of the trailer tongue to:

    (a) the trailer axles.
    (b) front wheels of the towing vehicle.
    (c) back wheels of the towing vehicle.
    (d) all four wheels of the towing vehicle.

12. When hitching a trailer the tongue weight should be:

    (a) as little as possible.
    (b) about one third the trailer axle weight.
    (c) 5 to 10 percent of the gross vehicle weight.
    (d) no maximum limit. The heavier, the better.

13. The maximum Gross Vehicle Weight when towing with a Class II hitch is:

    (a) 500 pounds.
    (b) 2,000 pounds.
    (c) 3,500 pounds.
    (d) 10 percent of GVW.

14. To steer the rear of the trailer to the left when backing, you must:

    (a) turn the top of the steering wheel to the left.
    (b) turn the bottom of the steering wheel to the right.
    (c) turn the bottom of the steering wheel to the left.
    (d) turn the bottom of the steering wheel opposite to which the trailer starts to turn.

15. Immersing a hot wheel hub of a trailer:

    (a) cools it.
    (b) causes water to enter it.
    (c) is apt to cause future trouble.
    (d) all of the above.

16. Riding in the boat on a trailer while moving is:

    (a) dangerous and illegal in many states.
    (b) permitted to balance the load.
    (c) permitted when traveling under 25 mph.
    (d) recommended if a rider has a communication link with the towing vehicle.

17. Trailers immersed in salt water should be:

    (a) rinsed off with fresh water as soon as possible.
    (b) hot-dip galvanized.
    (c) extra strong.
    (d) both a and b.

18. To avoid damage during long-term storage, trailer tires should:

    (a) have the weight taken off them.
    (b) not require any special care.
    (c) be overinflated.
    (d) be underinflated.

Appendices

CHAPMAN REFERENCES

Chapman Piloting Seamanship & Small Boat Handling
62nd Edition
by Elbert S. Maloney
Hearst Marine Books

	Chapter	Pages
1—Boat Handling and Elementary Seamanship	3	67–69
	4	83–99
	8	160–162
	9	188–209
	12	252–275
Boating Types and Terms	1	16–39
2—Registration	2	51–52
Equipment Regulations	3	61–81
Safe Boating	4	96–97
Operation	8	180–181
Marlinspike Seamanship	13	276–295
Weather	14	297–327
3—Charts and Aids	18	393–425
	22	501–519
Coastal Boating	15	328–349
Inland	21	485–497
	22	512–513
Great Lakes Boating	2	54–56
	6	119
	18	417–418
	21	498–499

4—	Basic Navigation	17	367–391
	Engine Maintenance	16	352–354
		23	523–532
		23	536–538
5—	Piloting	17	376–391
		19	427–443
		20	444–483
	Sailing	10	211–239
6—	Navigation Rules	6	117–133
		7	135–151
	Radiotelephone	4	84–86
		24	545–558
	Trailering	8	153–176

GLOSSARY

ABAFT Behind, toward a vessel's stern.

ABEAM Off to the side, amidships, at right angles to the fore and aft line.

ADRIFT Unattached to shore or bottom, floating out of control.

AFT At, near, or toward the stern.

AGROUND Touching or stuck on the bottom.

AHEAD In front of the vessel, forward; opposite of astern.

ALOFT Above deck, usually in the rigging.

AMIDSHIPS In or near the middle of the boat.

ANCHOR Device used to secure boat to bottom of body of water.

ASTERN At any point behind the boat, backward.

ATHWART At right angles to the fore-and-aft line of a vessel.

BACK Change in direction of the wind in a counterclockwise direction. *See* VEER.

BACKSTAY Part of standing rigging, usually cable, that supports the mast from aft.

BALLAST Weight carried low in a boat to improve trim or stability.

BATTEN Stiffening strip placed in leech of sail. Also, a wooden strip fastened over seam to stop leakage.

BEACON Anything that serves as a signal or indication for guidance or warning. A fixed (non-floating) aid to navigation.

BEAM The extreme width of a vessel. A horizontal, athwartship support for the deck.

BEAR OFF Steer away from the wind, shore, or any object.

BEARING Horizontal direction of an object from an observer, expressed as an angle from a reference direction (e.g., compass bearing, true bearing, relative bearing). Also, a device for supporting a rotating shaft with minimum friction, which may take the form of a metal sleeve (a bushing), a set of ball bearings (a roller bearing), or a set of pins around a shaft (a needle bearing).

BELAY Secure a line without a knot or hitch. Also, command to stop or cease action.

BELOW Beneath the deck.

BEND Secure a sail fast to a spar or stay. Also, knot to secure a line to another line or object such as an anchor.

BIGHT Open or closed loop in a line or rope.

BILGE The lowest part of the ship's interior.

BITTER END The inboard end of a line, chain, or cable. The end made fast to the vessel, as opposed to the "working end," which may be attached to an anchor, cleat, other vessel, etc.

BOLLARD Stout post on wharf or pier for securing mooring lines.

BOOM Spar used to extend and control foot of fore-and-aft sail.

BOW The forward end of a boat.

BROACH The turning of a boat broadside to the wind or waves, subjecting it to possible capsizing.

BULKHEAD A vertical partition or wall.

BULWARK The portion of hull extending above the deck.

CAPSIZE To turn over, upset.

CAST OFF To let go a line, as to cast off a bowline.

CENTERBOARD A hinged board that can be lowered through a slot in the keel to reduce leeway.

CHINE A line formed by the intersection of the sides and bottom of a flat or V-bottomed boat.

CHOCK A fitting to guide a line or cable. Also, a wedge or block to keep an object from moving.

CLEAT A fitting—secured to the deck, mast, or spar—having two projecting horns to which lines are made fast.

CLEW Aft, lower corner of a sail.

CLOSE HAULED Sailing as directly into the wind as possible. Also, on-the-wind.

COAMING A raised section around a hatch or cockpit to keep out water.

COCKPIT Well or sunken space in the deck.

COME ABOUT Significant course change; in sailing, to bring the bow through the wind or tack.

COMPASS ERROR Combined effect of variation and deviation.

COURSE The direction in which a boat is steered.

DECK The nautical equivalent of a floor.

DEVIATION Disturbing effect of boat's magnetic field upon its compass.

DINGHY A small open boat used as tender and lifeboat for a yacht.

DOCK The area of water in which a boat rests between two landing piers or wharves.

DRAFT The depth of water needed to float a boat. Also, the fullness or "belly" of a sail.

DROGUE Object streamed from boat to decrease speed; sea anchor.

FAIRLEAD Fitting to route control lines or cables.

FAIRWAY A navigable channel in a body of water.

FATHOM A unit of length used in measuring water depth. One fathom equals 6 feet.

FENDER A protector hung over the side between the boat and a pier, or another vessel.

FLARE The outward curve of the hull toward the deck.

FLUKE Flattened end of an anchor arm which bites into the ground.

FORE Prefix denoting at, near, or toward the bow.

FOUL Not clear; jammed.

FOUL GROUND A place not suitable for anchoring.

FREEBOARD The vertical distance from the water surface to the lowest point where unwanted water could come aboard.

GAFF Spar which supports the upper side of a fore-and-aft four-sided sail. Also, long-handled hook to bring fish aboard.

GAFF RIG Any sailboat with a four-sided mainsail.

GEAR The general name for all nonpermanent nautical equipment, including crew's clothing and personal effects.

GIVE-WAY BOAT One that does not have the right-of-way and should avoid the stand-on boat.

GROUND TACKLE An anchor and anchoring gear.

GUNWALE The part of a vessel where hull and deck meet. (Pronounced "gun'l.")

HALYARD Line for hoisting sails or flags.

HATCH A closable opening in the deck.

HEAD A boat's toilet. Also the upper corner of a triangular sail. The foremost part of a vessel.

HEADING Direction in which a boat is pointing at a given moment.

HEAVE To throw, as to heave a line ashore. The rise and fall of a vessel in a seaway.

HEAVE TO To bring a vessel to a position where she will maintain little or no headway, usually with the bow into the wind or nearly so.

HEEL The leaning of a vessel to one side such as caused by the wind.

HELM The apparatus by which a vessel is steered, including the rudder.

HULL The basic structure and shell of a boat.

JIB Triangular sail set on a stay forward of the mast.

JIBE Changing sail from one side to another with wind astern.

KEEL The main structural member of a hull (backbone); underwater extension of hull to increase lateral resistance and stability.

KNOT A general term for securing a line to an object, another line, or itself. Also, a unit of speed equal to one nautical mile per hour.

LEE SHORE One onto which wind or current could force a boat.

LEE SIDE The side away or opposite that from which the wind blows. Also, an area sheltered from the wind.

LEEWARD Direction away from the wind; downwind. (Pronounced "loo-rd.")

LEEWAY Sidewise movement of a boat through the water, caused by wind or current.

LIE TO *See* HEAVE TO.

LIST The leaning of a vessel to one side, caused by misplaced gear or shifting cargo.

LUFF Forward edge of a fore-and-aft sail.

LUFFING To luff or luff up is to head into the wind, causing sails to flutter.

MAINSAIL Boat's principle sail, set aft of mainmast.

MARLINSPIKE SEAMANSHIP General knowledge of knots, bends, hitches, splices, and care of rope.

NAUTICAL MILE A unit of distance equal to one minute of latitude and approximately equal to 6,076.1 feet, or 1.15 statute miles.

OUTHAUL Line or device used to tension the foot of a sail.

PAINTER A line tied to the bow of a dinghy for towing or making fast.

PAY OUT Slacken or let out a line.

PENDANT Short rope serving as an extension of a line, chain, cable with descriptive name based on use, e.g., mooring pendant.

PENNANT A tapering flag.

PIER A loading platform extending out from the shore.

PITCHPOLE Capsize end over end.

PORT The left side of a boat when facing the bow. Also, toward the boat's left. Also, opening in a boat's side (e.g., portlight). Also, harbor.

QUARTER Afterpart of a vessel's side (port quarter, starboard quarter).

REACH A point of sail between close-hauled and a run. Also, a distance, or fetch.

RELATIVE BEARING Direction of an object relative to a boat's heading.

SCOPE The ratio of the length of the payed out anchor line (rode) to the height of the chock above the bottom of the body of water.

SCUPPER An opening in a deck or cockpit permitting water to drain out.

SEA ANCHOR Device used for slowing a boat down. *See* DROGUE.

SHEET Line used to position a sail relative to the wind.

SHROUD Standing rigging that supports a mast laterally.

SKEG An extension of the keel for protection of propeller and rudder.

SLACK WATER Minimum velocity of a tidal current (sometimes abbreviated "slack").

SPEED Rate of motion.

STAND-ON BOAT One that has the right-of-way and should maintain her course and speed.

STARBOARD The right side of a vessel, looking forward.

STAYS Standing rigging that supports a mast fore and aft.

STEM The leading edge of a vessel's hull.

STERN The after end of a vessel.

SWAMP To fill with water, but not to founder.

TOPSIDE On or above a weather deck, i.e., a deck wholly exposed to the elements.

TOPSIDES The sides of a vessel between the waterline and the deck. *See* FREEBOARD.

TRANSOM The athwartship portion of a hull at the stern.

TRIM The longitudinal balance of a boat. If either the bow or stern is depressed, the vessel is said to be down by the bow or down by the stern. Also, to adjust the set of a sail.

VEER Wind veers when its direction changes clockwise.

WAKE The disturbed water following a moving vessel.

WASH The rush or sweeping of waves on a bank, shore, or vessel.

WAY Movement of a vessel through the water such as headway, sternway, or leeway.

WHARF Man-made structure parallel to the shoreline, for loading, unloading, or making fast.

WHIPPING Method of binding the end of a rope with small twine.

WINDWARD The direction from which the wind is blowing. (Pronounced "wind'ard.")

YAW To swing off course, caused by the action of waves or bad steering.

Boaters in Canada are governed by different laws and regulations than those for U.S. owners and skippers. In most cases the Canadian regulations do not apply to U.S. boaters temporarily visiting in Canadian waters.

Boat Licenses

Licenses are required for all vessels not exceeding 15 registered tons (and each passenger craft not exceeding 20 registered tons) equipped with a motor or motors of 7.5kW (10 hp) or more. Pleasure vessels over 20 tons must re-register. Any Canada Customs office can provide a license free on request. Before the boat is operated, the license number must be marked in block characters, not less than 75 mm high and in a color that contrasts with the background, on each side of the bow or on a board permanently attached as close to the bow as possible. The number must be clearly visible from each side. Registered vessels must be marked in block characters 103 mm high.

Construction Standards

Canadian Small Vessel Regulations require that certain classes of boats be built to specific current safety standards covering minimum requirements for hull construction, flotation, ventilation of explosive fumes, and fuel and electrical systems.

Basically, these standards apply to power-driven pleasure boats not longer than 6 meters and without an enclosed cabin for sleeping, and to *all* pleasure craft, regardless of length or type of accommodation, if fitted with one or more gasoline engines for propulsion or generation of electrical power.

Boats that meet the prescribed standards will have an appropriate decal prominently displayed.

Safe Loading and Engine Power

Canadian law requires every pleasure boat 5 meters or less in length, powered with an outboard motor or motors of 7kW (10 hp) or more, to carry a plate issued by Transport Canada stating the recommended maximum load and engine power. The recommended load capacity includes weight of passengers, engine, fuel and fuel tanks, and all other equipment.

Applications for these plates can be obtained from any Canada Customs or Coast Guard Ship Safety office. The completed form and appropriate fee should be sent to Canadian Coast Guard, Ship Safety, Place de Ville, Ottawa, Ontario K1A 0N7.

Ventilation

Canadian Small Vessel Regulations require any enclosed space in which an inboard gasoline engine is installed to be ventilated efficiently by suitable ventilators and an exhaust fan. Although this specific regulation applies only to inboard engines, all enclosed spaces in both inboard and outboard powerboats should be well ventilated if they contain fuel tanks or other containers of gasoline.

The number, size, and other details of ventilation ducts and fans are generally the same as the U.S. requirements.

Reckless Operation

All Rules of the Road must be obeyed, and the operation of any craft must not be "reckless."

Anyone operating a boat, air-cushion vehicle, water skis, surfboard, or any towed object in a manner dangerous to navigation, life, or limb is guilty of an indictable offense and liable to imprisonment or punishment on summary conviction.

Under the Criminal Code of Canada, this offense includes:

- operating a vessel when impaired,
- towing a person on water skis after dark or without another person keeping watch, and
- failing to stop at the scene of an accident.

Charges can be laid against a reckless operator by "laying an information," a procedure that requires making a sworn statement before a Magistrate or Justice of the Peace.

EQUIPMENT REQUIREMENTS FOR CANADIAN BOATS

The list of required equipment for boats licensed in Canada is more extensive than it is for their counterparts in the United States. Canadian craft are divided into five classes based on overall length in metric units.

Vessels Not Longer Than 5.5 Meters

1. One approved small vessel life jacket, or approved PFD, or approved lifesaving cushion for each person on board.
2. Two oars and rowlocks or two paddles.
3. One bailer or one manual pump.
4. One Class B-I fire extinguisher if the vessel has an inboard motor, permanently fixed or built-in fuel tanks, or a cooking or heating appliance that burns liquid or gaseous fuel.*

*Details on various acceptable fire extinguishers and pyrotechnic distress signals will be found in the *Canadian Coast Guard Boating Handbook.*

5. Navigation lights, if permanently fitted, that comply with the Collision Regulations.
6. Some means of making an efficient sound signal.

Vessels Longer Than 5.5 Meters but Not Longer Than 8 Meters

1. One approved small vessel life jacket or approved PFD for each person on board.
2. Two oars and rowlocks or two paddles, or one anchor with not less than 15 m of cable, rope, or chain.
3. One bailer or one manual pump.
4. One Class B-I fire extinguisher if the vessel is power-driven, or has a cooking or heating appliance that burns liquid or gaseous fuel.*
5. One throwing device that may be either an approved lifesaving cushion, a buoyant heaving line (recommended minimum length 15 m), or an approved life buoy 508, 610, or 762 mm in diameter.
6. Six approved pyrotechnic distress signals (flares) of which at least three must be Types A, B, or C, and the remaining three Types A, B, C, or D. (Note: These are not required if the vessel is engaged in or preparing for racing competition and has no sleeping accommodation, or is operating in a river, canal, or lake in which the boat can never be more than one mile from shore, or is propelled solely by oars or paddles.)
7. Navigation lights, if permanently fitted, that comply with the requirements of the Collision Regulations.
8. Some means of making an efficient sound signal.

Vessels Longer Than 8 Meters but Not Longer Than 12 Meters

1. One approved life jacket or PFD for each person on board. (Note: Sailing vessels without an enclosed sleeping cabin may instead carry one approved PFD for each person on board.)
2. One approved life buoy 610 or 762 mm in diameter.
3. One buoyant heaving line at least 15 m long.
4. One bilge pump and one manual bailer.
5. Twelve approved pyrotechnic distress signals of which at least six must be Types A, B, or C, and the remaining six Types A, B, C, or D.
6. One anchor with at least 15 m of cable, rope, or chain.
7. One Class B-II fire extinguisher if the vessel is power-driven, or has a cooking or heating appliance that burns liquid or gaseous fuel.
8. Navigation lights and sound signaling apparatus that permit the vessel to comply with the Collision Regulations.

Vessels Longer Than 12 Meters but Not Longer Than 20 Meters

1. One approved standard life jacket or one approved small vessel life jacket for each person on board.
2. One approved life buoy 762 mm in diameter, or two approved life buoys 610 mm in diameter.
3. One buoyant heaving line at least 15 m long.
4. Twelve approved pyrotechnic distress signals of which at least six must be Types A, B, or C, and the remaining six Types A, B, C, or D.

5. One anchor with at least 15 m of cable, rope, or chain.
6. Two fire buckets or other effective means of carrying water to any part of the vessel to extinguish a fire.
7. (a) A manual or power-driven pump outside the machinery space with one fire hose and nozzle that can direct a jet of water into any part of the vessel.
   (b) Two Class B-II fire extinguishers, one of which is next to the sleeping cabin entrance and the other next to the machinery space entrance.
8. Efficient bilge-pumping system.
9. One additional Class B-II fire extinguisher if the vessel is power-driven, or has a cooking or heating appliance that burns liquid or gaseous fuel.
10. One fire ax.
11. Navigation lights and sound signaling apparatus that permit the vessel to comply with the Collision Regulations.

Other Vessels

Sailboards and water scooters must have one approved PFD for each person.

Vessels longer than 20 m require larger amounts of equipment as specified in the *Canadian Coast Guard Boating Handbook.*

Radar Reflectors

Every pleasure boat shorter than 20 m *or* constructed primarily of materials other than metal must have a passive radar reflector that provides a response in the 3-cm marine radar band equivalent to an effective reflecting area not less than 10 m^2 through 360 degrees; this must be located, if possible, at least 4 m above the water.

ANSWERS TO THE STUDY QUESTIONS

SECTION I

Boat Handling and Elementary Seamanship

1 (d)
2 (a)
3 (c)
4 (b)
5 (a)
6 (c)
7 (d)
8 (d)
9 (b)
10 (c)
11 (c)
12 (d)
13 (a)
14 (b)
15 (d)
16 (a)
17 (b)
18 (a)
19 (c)
20 (b)
21 (a)
22 (a)

Boat Types

1 (d)
2 (b)
3 (c)
4 (d)
5 (c)
6 (b)
7 (c)
8 (d)
9 (c)
10 (c)

11 (c)
12 (b)
13 (c)
14 (c)
15 (d)
16 (a)
17 (d)
18 (c)
19 (b)

SECTION II

Regulations, Safe Boating, and Equipment

1 (b)
2 (b)
3 (a)
4 (d)
5 (b)
6 (c)
7 (c)
8 (c)
9 (a)
10 (d)
11 (d)
12 (b)
13 (c)
14 (d)
15 (d)
16 (d)
17 (a)
18 (c)
19 (b)
20 (b)
21 (b)
22 (d)
23 (b)
24 (a)
25 (c)
26 (b)
27 (d)
28 (b)
29 (d)

Marlinspike

1 (c)
2 (b)
3 (c)
4 (d)

5 (b)
6 (c)
7 (b)
8 (d)
9 (a)
10 (d)

Weather

1 (d)
2 (a)
3 (c)
4 (b)
5 (d)
6 (b)
7 (c)
8 (d)
9 (c)
10 (b)
11 (d)
12 (d)
13 (a)
14 (d)

SECTION III

Aids to Navigation

1 (c)
2 (d)
3 (d)
4 (c)
5 (d)
6 (a)
7 (a)
8 (d)
9 (c)
10 (b)
11 (b)
12 (c)
13 (c)
14 (b)
15 (d)
16 (a)
17 (b)
18 (d)
19 (d)
20 (b)

Coastal Boating

1 (c)
2 (d)
3 (a)

	4	(d)
	5	(a)
	6	(d)
	7	(d)
	8	(d)
	9	(c)
	10	(a)
Inland Boating	1	(a)
	2	(d)
	3	(b)
	4	(a)
	5	(b)
	6	(d)
	7	(b)
	8	(c)
	9	(b)
	10	(c)
Great Lakes Boating	1	(d)
	2	(a)
	3	(b)
	4	(c)
	5	(b)
	6	(a)
	7	(b)
	8	(c)

SECTION IV

Basic Navigation	1	(b)
	2	(d)
	3	(a)
	4	(a)
	5	(c)
	6	(c)
	7	(c)
	8	(d)
	9	(b)
	10	(c)
	11	(b)
	12	(c)
	13	(a)
	14	(d)
	15	(d)
	16	(a)
	17	(c)
	18	(c)
	19	(a)
	20	(b)

Engine Troubleshooting

1 (d)
2 (c)
3 (b)
4 (b)
5 (c)
6 (c)
7 (a)
8 (b)
9 (a)

SECTION V

Piloting

1(a)—10.0 kn 1(b)—10.0 kn 1(c)—13.2 kn, 102 min 2(a)—4.6 nm 2(b)—16.0 nm, 84 min 2(c)—11.0 nm 3(a)—58 min 3(b)—74 min = 1 hr 14 min 3(c)—54 min 4(a)—0835 4(b)—2351 4(c)—0625 4(d)—1534 5(a)—12:07 a.m. 5(b)—10:21 p.m. 5(c)—6:38 a.m. 5(d)—6:38 p.m. 6(a)—1238 6(b)—0038 6(c)—1108 6(d)—0044 6(e)—0054 7(a)—2 hr 17 min 7(b)—2 hr 34 min 7(c)—46 min 7(d)—18 min 8(a)—260 8(b)—070 8(c)—035 8(d)—320 9(a)—5W 9(b)—11E 9(c)—10E 9(d)—5W 10(a)—L 41° 30.7´ N Lo 67° 57.9´ W 10(b)—L 41° 27.5´ N Lo 67° 58.9´ W 10(c)—L 41° 33.4´ N Lo 68° 06.1´ W 11(a)—130 11(b)—119 11(c)—8.6 nm 11(d)—1 hr 26 min 11(e)—1026 12(a)—080 12(b)—069 12(c)—7.0 nm 12(d)—1 hr 10 min 12(e)—1045 12(f)—L 41° 28.1´ N Lo 68° 01.0´ w

SECTION V

Sailing

1 (c)
2 (d)
3 (b)
4 (a)
5 (c)
6 (d)
7 (b)

8	(d)
9	(d)
10	(c)
11	(b)
12	(c)

SECTION VI

Navigation Rules

1	(a)
2	(c)
3	(b)
4	(d)
5	(c)
6	(d)
7	(d)
8	(d)
9	(c)
10	(d)
11	(a)
12	(c)
13	(b)
14	(c)
15	(b)
16	(d)
17	(c)
18	(c)
19	(a)
20	(c)
21	(a)

Marine Radiotelephone

1	(d)
2	(c)
3	(d)
4	(b)
5	(c)
6	(b)
7	(d)
8	(b)

Boat Trailering

1	(c)
2	(b)
3	(c)
4	(d)
5	(c)
6	(a)
7	(a)

8 (d)
9 (a)
10 (c)
11 (d)
12 (c)
13 (c)
14 (c)
15 (d)
16 (a)
17 (d)
18 (a)